**CHRISTMAS IS
COMING! 1986**

CHRISTMAS IS COMING! 1986

**Compiled and Edited
by Linda Martin Stewart**

**Designed and Illustrated
by David Morrison**

Oxmoor
House®

© 1986 by Oxmoor House, Inc.
Book Division of Southern Progress Corporation
P.O. Box 2463, Birmingham, Alabama 35201

Library of Congress Catalog Card Number:
84-63030

ISBN: 0-8487-0688-9
ISSN: 0883-9077

Manufactured in the United States of America
Second Printing

Executive Editor: Candace N. Conard
Production Manager: Jerry Higdon
Associate Production Manager: Rick Litton
Art Director: Bob Nance

Christmas Is Coming! 1986

Editor: Linda Martin Stewart
Editorial Assistant: Lenda Wyatt
Copy Chief: Mary Jean Haddin
Photographers: Jim Bathie, Beth Maynor,
   Courtland W. Richards
Assistant Art Director: David Morrison

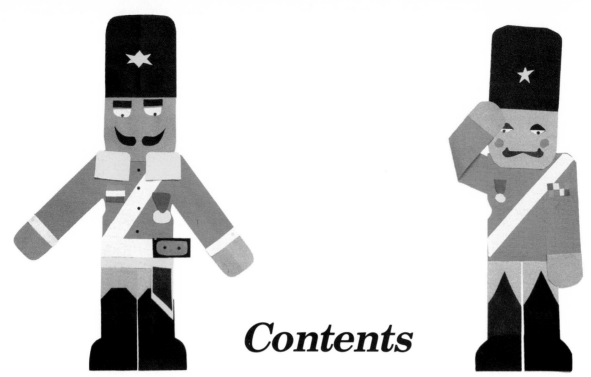

Contents

A Word to Parents

Although reading has always been a hobby of mine, I must confess that before joining the ranks as an editor, I was unaware of how books came into being. Little did I know that books are like babies—they're born! To produce *Christmas Is Coming!* takes many months—about a year's worth—and a multitude of steps and stages. One giant step is completing the photography.

Photographing the cover for *Christmas Is Coming! 1986* was quite an experience—and one that those of us involved will not soon forget! Initial plans for the snowy scene included a dog, one of undetermined breeding, with a face that belongs in the movies. Dressed in a holiday sweater, the pup was to sit contentedly while two children put the finishing touches on their snowman. Not so! After two photography sessions, three dogs, a case of dog biscuits, and the last-ditch efforts of a professional dog trainer, we concluded that no dog with sense would sit in a roomful of strangers, beneath flashing lights and falling plastic snow, and smile for the camera. We sent the dogs and the biscuits home and moved to plan B: photographing just the snowman and the children.

I would like to tip my hat to the cover kids (who are, by the way, brother and sister) for being such terrific sports. They got hot, and they must have gotten tired, but they continued to cooperate and never complained. And while I'm at it, I'd like to compliment the rest of the children in *Christmas Is Coming! 1986*, too. Not one is a professional model, but all are first-rate. Each was charming and a delight to work with!

Within the pages of this year's *Christmas Is Coming!*, youngsters will again find plenty to keep them busy while waiting for Santa to come. As you glance over the projects in Children's Workshop, notice that suggestions (Before You Start) or words of caution (For Safety's Sake) occasionally precede the instructions. Also note that at the bottom of the first page of each project, there is a level rating of 1, 2, or 3, with Level 1 indicating the quickest, easiest projects, and Level 3 the most difficult ones or those calling for adult supervision. The projects within Level 2 are easy but call for a certain skill, such as sewing, or for extra time and patience. Please understand that these ratings are intended only as a guide, to help you and your children decide which projects are suitable for them to make.

While the children are sleeping all snug in their beds, grown-ups can turn to Parents' Workshop, and lend old Santa a helping hand. Here you'll find an abundance of gifts to make for kids—from bear chairs to cradles to cross-stitched long underwear, there's something for every youngster you know.

Now gather up the kids and have a long look inside this exciting new book. Christmas is coming! Let's get busy and make it an extra-merry one!

Linda Martin Stewart

CHILDREN'S WORKSHOP
Happy Holiday Crafts

Powder-Puff Snowmen

Use snowy white puffs to make these folks. Cover their ears so they won't get cold!

You will need:
white glue
4 small white powder puffs
hole punch
scraps of felt
scissors
rickrack
4 small pom-poms
ribbon bow
scrap of fabric for scarf
pencil
tracing paper
ribbon

1. Glue the edge of one powder puff over the edge of another powder puff to make the snowman's head and body. Let the glue dry.

2. Use a hole punch to make felt circles for eyes and buttons. Glue them in place. Cut out a carrot nose and glue it in place

3. For earmuffs, glue a piece of rickrack and two pom-poms on the snowman's head. Let the glue dry.

4. For Mrs. Snowman, glue on the ribbon bow.

5. For Mr. Snowman, cut a strip for a scarf from the scrap of fabric. Tie the scarf around the snowman's neck. Glue the scarf, if you need to, to keep it in place.

   Trace the patterns for the broom on tracing paper. Cut out the patterns and draw around them on felt. Cut out the felt pieces and glue them together. When the glue is dry, glue the broom to the back of Mr. Snowman.

6. Cut a piece of ribbon for a hanger. Glue the ends of the ribbon to the back of the snowman. Let the glue dry.

Broom

5

Shiny Shapes

Making these ornaments is as easy as counting one—two—three!

You will need:
fine-tip marker
tracing paper
scissors
vinyl in different colors
hole punch
toothpick
white glue
ribbon

1. Trace the patterns for the heart, star, and tree on tracing paper. Cut out the patterns and draw around them on vinyl. Cut out the vinyl ornaments.

2. To make balls for the tree, punch holes in scraps of vinyl. Using the toothpick, put tiny dots of glue on the front of the tree. Place the balls on the dots of glue. Let the glue dry.

3. Punch a hole in the top of each ornament. For a hanger, pull the ends of a ribbon through the hole and tie a knot.

Glitter Birds

These silver birds are sweet as can be. And how they will sparkle on your Christmas tree!

You will need:
felt-tip marker
6″ square of tracing paper
clear tape
6″ square of cardboard
plastic wrap
white glue
tinsel cord (about 19″ for each ornament)
toothpick
glitter
scissors
aluminum foil
ribbon
sequins
straight pin
fishing line

1. Using the felt-tip marker and tracing paper, trace the pattern.

2. Tape the tracing to the piece of cardboard. Cover the tracing and cardboard with plastic wrap. Tape the edges of the plastic wrap to the back of the cardboard.

3. Trace the design with a thin line of glue. Allow the glue to dry for several minutes.

4. Place the tinsel cord along the lines of glue. Hold the cord in place until the glue is slightly dry. Let the glue dry.

5. Fill the area inside the cord with glue, using a toothpick to spread the glue. Sprinkle glitter over the glue. Let the glue dry for several days.

6. When the glue is completely dry, gently peel the bird from the plastic wrap. Cut a beak from aluminum foil. Cut a piece of ribbon and tie it into a bow. Glue the beak, the bow, and a sequin eye in place. Let the glue dry.

7. Poke a hole in the top of the ornament with a straight pin. Pull a piece of fishing line through the hole and tie the ends to make a hanger.

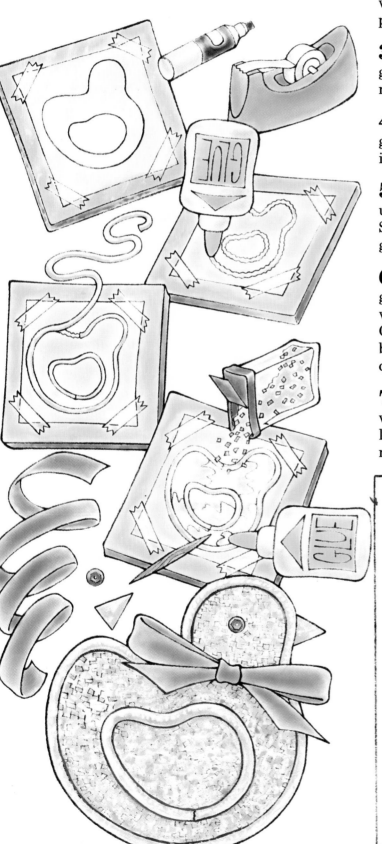

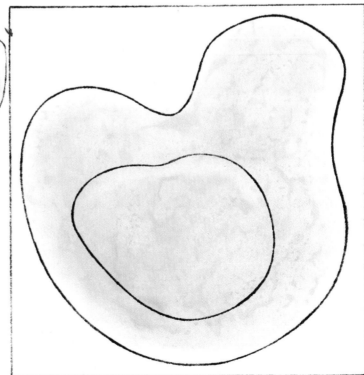

Dream Cones

Strawberry, lemon, or lime? Pick your favorite flavor. Turn sugar cones into dream cones and hang them on your tree.

You will need:
paper cup (5-ounce size works well)
scissors
sugar cone
colored tissue paper
measuring spoons
white glue
water
foil pie pan
1 (2¼″) plastic foam ball
glitter
narrow ribbon

1. Turn the paper cup upside down. In the bottom of the cup, cut a hole that is big enough to hold the sugar cone. Stand the sugar cone in the hole.

2. Tear the tissue paper into little pieces that are about the size of a half-dollar. Mix three tablespoons of glue with three tablespoons of water in the foil pie pan.

3. Dip a piece of the tissue paper into the glue mixture and smooth it onto the ball. Cover the whole ball with pieces of tissue paper that have been dipped in glue. Sprinkle the ball with glitter.

4. Spread glue around the inside edge of the sugar cone. Gently push the ball into the cone. Let the dream cone dry.

5. Cut two pieces of ribbon. Fold one ribbon in half. Glue the ends onto the top of the ball to make a hanger. Tie the other ribbon into a little bow and glue it to the ball for decoration. Let the glue dry.

11

Surprise-in-a-Box

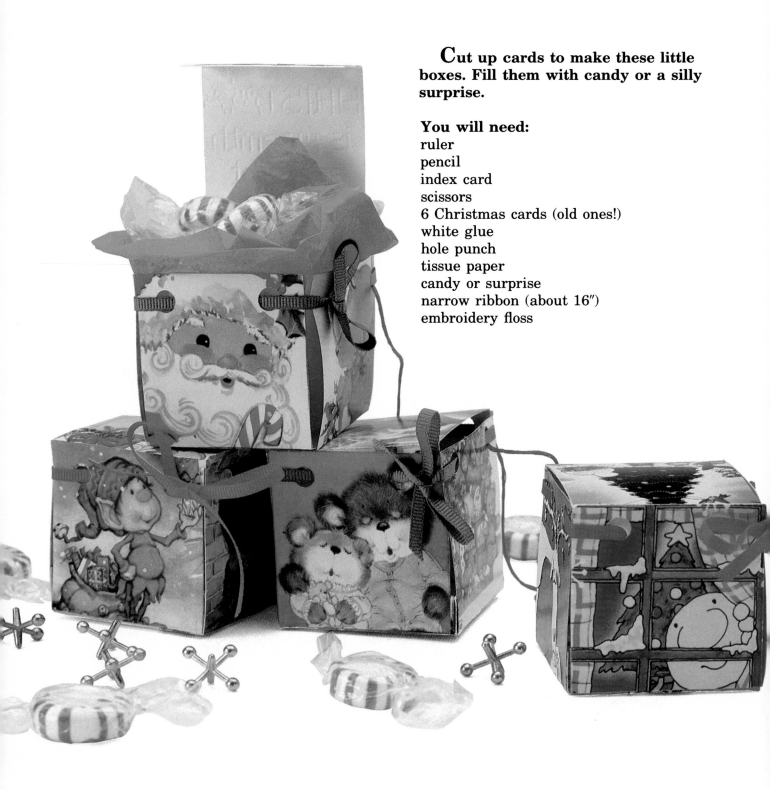

Cut up cards to make these little boxes. Fill them with candy or a silly surprise.

You will need:
ruler
pencil
index card
scissors
6 Christmas cards (old ones!)
white glue
hole punch
tissue paper
candy or surprise
narrow ribbon (about 16″)
embroidery floss

Sides

Bottom

Bottom

Top

1. Using a ruler, measure and draw a 2″ square on an index card. Cut out the square to use as a pattern for drawing squares around pictures on the Christmas cards.

2. Draw a square on four different Christmas cards. Cut out the squares. These will be the sides of the box.

3. For the bottom of the box, draw a square on a Christmas card. Draw a ½″ tab on each side of the square. Cut out the square with the tabs attached. Fold up the tabs.

4. For the top of the box, draw a square on a Christmas card. Draw a ½″ tab on the side of the square that is at the top of the picture. On the side of the square that is at the bottom of the picture, draw a 1″ tab. Cut out the square with the tabs attached. Fold down the tabs.

5. Glue the sides of the box to the tabs on the box bottom. Glue the ½″ tab that is on the box top to the top of one of the sides. Let the glue dry.

6. Using a hole punch, punch two holes in each side of the box, about ¼″ down from the top. Punch two holes in the 1″ tab that is on the box top, making sure that these holes line up with the two holes that you punched in the front of the box.

7. If you're making the box for a gift, place a small piece of tissue paper inside the box. Fill the box with candy or a small surprise.

8. Close the top of the box with the tab inside. Lace a piece of ribbon through the holes and tie a bow.

9. To make a hanger, pull a piece of embroidery floss through one of the holes and tie the ends.

Picture-Perfect Wreaths

Somebody would love to have a
picture of you. Can you guess who?

You will need:
pencil
coffee cup (about 3½" across)
felt
pinking shears
top to baby-food jar
Tacky Glue
scissors
ribbon bow
sequins
toothpick (for picking up sequins)
picture
ribbon for hanger

1. Draw around the coffee cup on felt. Using the pinking shears, cut out the felt circle.

2. Place the jar top in the center of the felt circle. Draw around the top. Using scissors, cut out the circle to make a wreath.

3. Glue the bow at the bottom of the wreath. Glue sequins for berries around the wreath. Let the glue dry.

4. Draw around the coffee cup on felt to make another circle. Use pinking shears to cut out the circle.

5. Glue the picture to the felt circle. At the top of the circle, glue the ends of the ribbon hanger. Put glue around the edges of the circle. Place the wreath on top. Let the glue dry.

How Dear!

Wouldn't Santa's reindeer get a kick out of these!

You will need:
pencil
dinner plate (about 10½″ across)
poster paper
scissors
12″ square of tan felt
glue stick
paper clips
tracing paper
6″ square of brown felt
ribbon for a hanger
ribbon bow
2 plastic wiggly-eyes
red pom-pom
tissue paper
candy

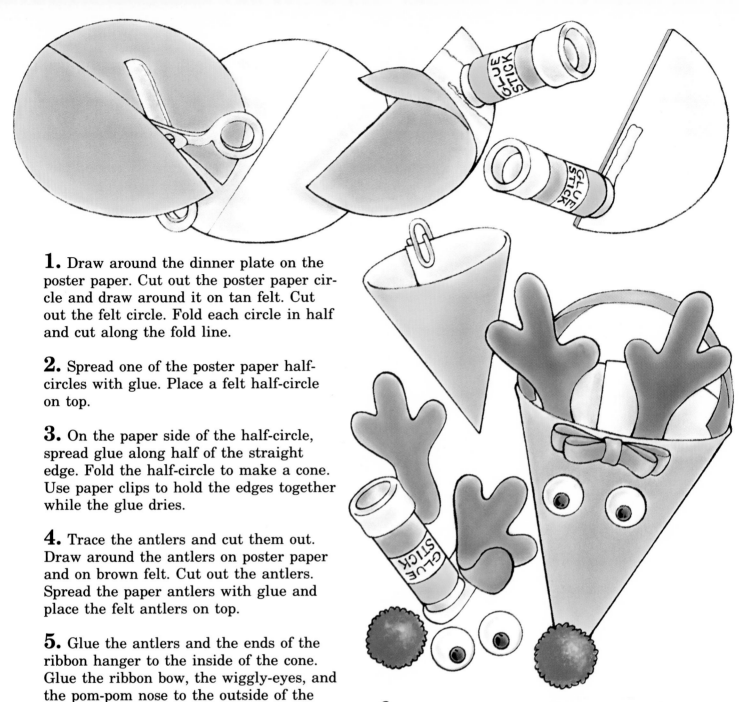

1. Draw around the dinner plate on the poster paper. Cut out the poster paper circle and draw around it on tan felt. Cut out the felt circle. Fold each circle in half and cut along the fold line.

2. Spread one of the poster paper half-circles with glue. Place a felt half-circle on top.

3. On the paper side of the half-circle, spread glue along half of the straight edge. Fold the half-circle to make a cone. Use paper clips to hold the edges together while the glue dries.

4. Trace the antlers and cut them out. Draw around the antlers on poster paper and on brown felt. Cut out the antlers. Spread the paper antlers with glue and place the felt antlers on top.

5. Glue the antlers and the ends of the ribbon hanger to the inside of the cone. Glue the ribbon bow, the wiggly-eyes, and the pom-pom nose to the outside of the cone. Use paper clips to hold the antlers, ribbon hanger, and bow while the glue dries.

6. Stuff tissue paper inside the cone. Fill the cone with candy and hang it on the tree.

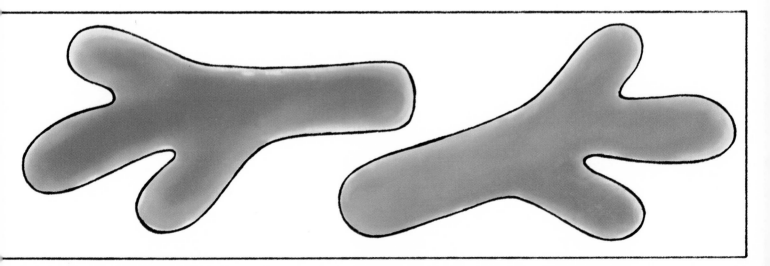

Waxen Wings

Make plenty of these heavenly ornaments. Tie them onto presents, a mobile, or your Christmas tree. See how the colors glow!

For safety's sake: Because you need an electric skillet for melting the wax to make these ornaments, you will need your mom to help. Skillets and melted wax can get burning hot! Be sure to keep the skillet at the lowest temperature setting and to put in just enough wax to coat the bottom of the skillet. Always use tweezers to place the pieces of paper for the ornaments in the wax and to take them out.

Making the Ornaments

You will need:
pencil
colored tissue paper
scissors
electric skillet (and your mom!)
potato peeler
bar of paraffin wax
white construction paper
tweezers
waxed paper
hole punch
narrow ribbons

1. Trace the patterns for the Moon with a Star, the Girl Angel, and the Boy Angel ornaments onto different colors of tissue paper. Cut out the pattern pieces, keeping separate piles for the three ornaments.

2. Ask your mom to turn the electric skillet to the lowest setting. Use a potato peeler to cut shavings from the bar of paraffin wax. Place only enough shavings in the skillet to coat the bottom and make it look shiny.

3. To make the Moon with a Star, cut a square of white construction paper that is a little bigger than the moon. Use tweezers to put the square in the skillet. Place the tissue paper moon on the square. Put the tissue paper star on the moon. Use tweezers to remove the ornament and to set it on a sheet of waxed paper.

4. To make either angel, cut a square of white construction paper that is a little bigger than the angel. Place the square in the skillet.

To make the Girl Angel, place (in this order) the tissue paper wings, face, dress, arms, hair, and halo on the square. Add the other pieces. Take out the ornament and set it on a sheet of waxed paper to dry.

To make the Boy Angel, place (in this order) the tissue paper wings, face, overalls, arms, hair, and halo on the square. Add the other pieces. Take out the ornament and set it on a sheet of waxed paper to dry.

5. When the ornaments are dry, trim the edges. Punch a hole in each ornament, looking at the patterns to see where to make the holes. Use ribbons for ties.

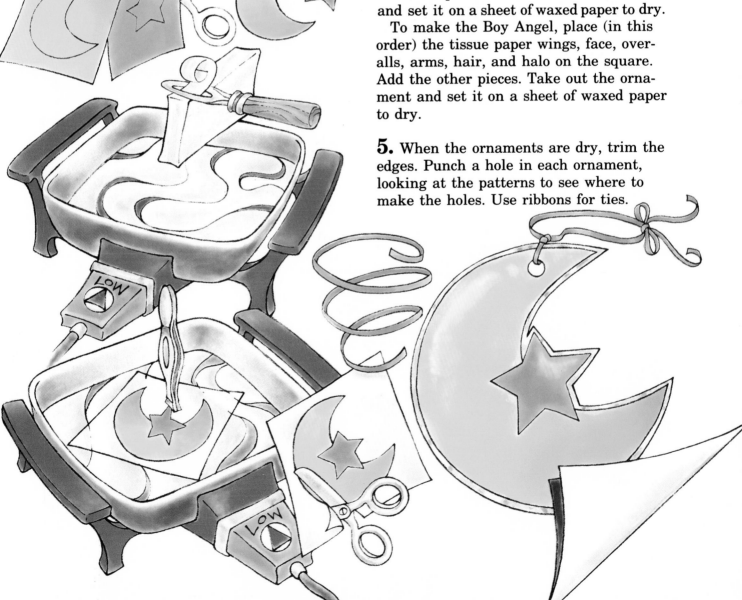

Making the Mobile

You will need:
acrylic paint
paper towels
9 inches (¼″) dowel
white glue
2 (⅝″) colored beads
2 yards of narrow ribbon
Moon, Girl Angel, and Boy Angel
 ornaments (without ribbons)

1. Put some paint on a paper towel. Rub the dowel with the paint. When the paint is dry, glue a colored bead onto each end of the dowel.

2. Cut the ribbon into pieces that are 12″, 16″, 20″, and 24″. Tie the 12″ ribbon around the middle of the dowel. Pull the ends of the ribbon through the hole in the Moon with a Star and tie a bow. In the same way, tie the Girl Angel onto the right side of the dowel, using the 16″ ribbon. Tie the Boy Angel onto the left side of the dowel, using the 20″ ribbon.

3. Tie the ends of the 24″ ribbon around the ends of the dowel. Use this ribbon for hanging the mobile.

A Bright Brigade

The more of these silly soldiers you make, the merrier they will look. Make an army! Parade them on a wall or the door to your room.

You will need:
construction paper in different colors
ruler
pencil
scissors
white glue

1. From black paper, cut one 6″ x 7″ piece for the hat, two 3″ x 7″ pieces for the boot tops, and two 3″ x 4″ pieces for the boot bottoms. From light brown paper, cut one 6″ x 6″ piece for the head and two 3″ x 3″ pieces for the hands. From red paper, cut two 3″ x 9″ pieces for the arms and one 6″ x 9″ piece for the body. From light blue paper, cut two 3″ x 10″ pieces for the legs.

2. Round off the top corners of the hat. Round off the bottom corners of the head. Glue the hat to the head.

3. Round off the top of the arms and the bottom of the hands. Glue the hands to the arms, the arms to the body, and the body to the head.

4. Cut the pieces of paper for the boots into boot shapes and glue them together. Glue the boots to the legs and the legs to the body.

5. Cut out eyes and a mustache. Cut out medals, a sash, and other trim. Glue the pieces in place.

23

Daffy Doormouse

Here's one mouse that Mom will welcome in the house! Tie him on a doorknob for a dandy decoration.

You will need:
felt-tip marker
small plate (about 7″ across)
green felt
scissors
ruler
hole punch
top to mayonnaise jar
Tacky Glue
top to baby-food jar
red felt
2 plastic wiggly-eyes
narrow ribbon
pom-pom

1. Draw around the plate on green felt. Cut out the felt circle. Using the hole punch, make holes that are 1″ apart around the circle, about 1″ from the edge.

2. Draw around the mayonnaise jar top four times on green felt. At the bottom of each felt circle, draw a tab that is 1″ long and 1½″ wide. Cut out the circles with the tabs attached.

3. Draw around the baby-food jar top two times on red felt. Cut out the felt circles.

4. For each ear, glue together two of the green felt circles with tabs. Glue a red felt circle on each ear.

5. Lay the ears in place on the felt circle with holes. Draw a line along the bottom of each ear tab. Cut along each line with your scissors.

6. Spread glue on the front of each ear tab. Put the tabs in the slits. Let the glue dry.

7. Glue on the wiggly-eyes. Cut six 2″ pieces of ribbon for whiskers. Put glue on one end of each ribbon. Glue the ribbon ends under the eyes. Glue a pom-pom nose on top of the ribbon ends. Let the glue dry.

8. Cut a piece of ribbon that is about 26″ long. Lace the ribbon through the holes.

9. Put the mouse on a doorknob. Pull the ends of the ribbon and tie a bow.

25

A Frosty Family

Mix up a batch of papier-mâché to build these snowmen. Give the grown-ups carrot noses. Give everyone a sunny smile!

You will need:
plastic foam balls
  for Mr. Snowman: 2½″, 3″, 4″
  for Mrs. Snowman: 2½″, 3″, 4″
  for Big Brother: 2¼″, 2¾″, 3¼″
  for Baby Sister: ¾″ (two for legs),
    1½″, 2¼″
4 craft sticks
2 toothpicks
twigs (for arms and the broom)
package of instant papier-mâché
paintbrushes
acrylic paint

scissors
felt in different colors
pencil
tracing paper
ruler
white glue
string
pair of baby socks

For Mr. Snowman: small feather, straw (from your mom's broom)

For Mrs. Snowman: rickrack, ribbon, small jingle bell, saucer, 6-ounce juice can, black hairnet

For Big Brother: small pom-pom

For Baby Sister: ribbon, 6″ square of white fabric, small safety pin

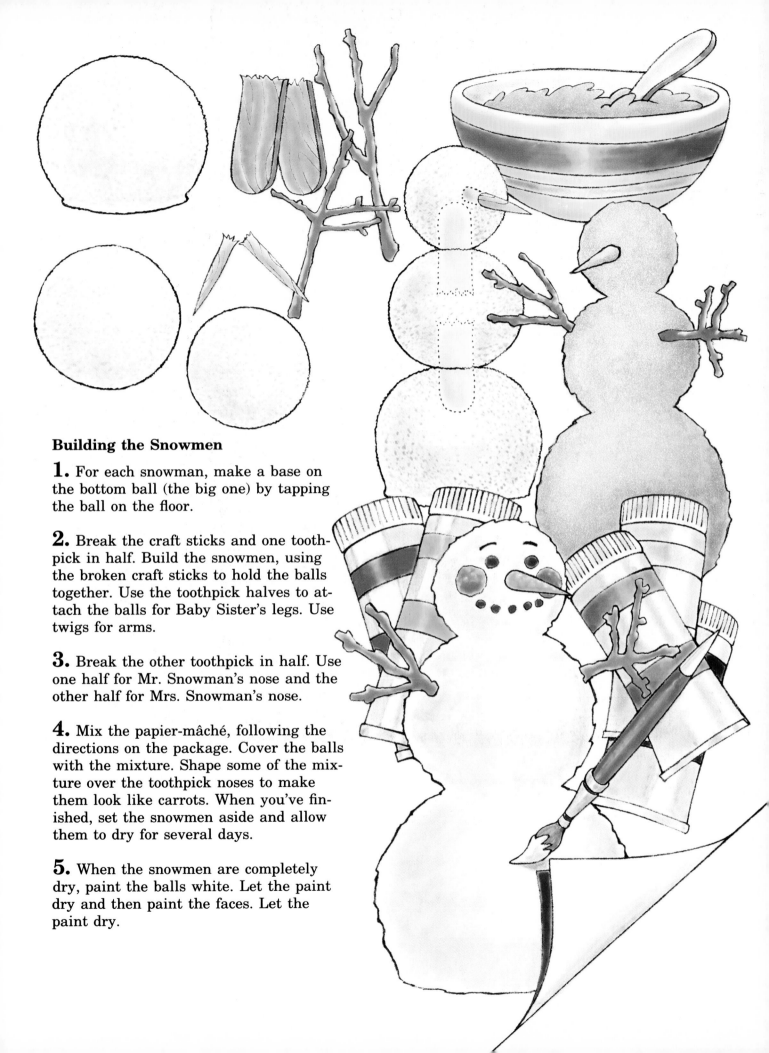

Building the Snowmen

1. For each snowman, make a base on the bottom ball (the big one) by tapping the ball on the floor.

2. Break the craft sticks and one toothpick in half. Build the snowmen, using the broken craft sticks to hold the balls together. Use the toothpick halves to attach the balls for Baby Sister's legs. Use twigs for arms.

3. Break the other toothpick in half. Use one half for Mr. Snowman's nose and the other half for Mrs. Snowman's nose.

4. Mix the papier-mâché, following the directions on the package. Cover the balls with the mixture. Shape some of the mixture over the toothpick noses to make them look like carrots. When you've finished, set the snowmen aside and allow them to dry for several days.

5. When the snowmen are completely dry, paint the balls white. Let the paint dry and then paint the faces. Let the paint dry.

Mr. Snowman

1. Cut a strip of felt for a scarf. Tie the scarf around Mr. Snowman's neck.

2. Trace the pattern for the vest. Cut out the pattern and draw around it on felt. Cut out the vest. Put it on the snowman.

3. Trace the pattern for the hat brim. Cut out the pattern and draw around it on felt.

   Cut around the outside of the felt brim. Then make a cut from the outside to the inside of the brim. Cut out the inside circle. Use this for the hat top.

4. Draw an 8½″ x 1¾″ rectangle on felt. Cut out the rectangle. Glue one end on top of the other to make the hat sides. Let the glue dry.

5. Glue the hat top to the hat sides. Pinch the edges together. Let the glue dry.

6. Glue the hat brim to the hat sides. Pinch the edges together. Glue one end of the brim over the other. Let the glue dry.

7. Cut an 8½″ x ⅜″ strip of felt for the hatband. Wrap the hatband around the hat and glue the ends to the back. Stick a feather in the hatband. Put the hat on the snowman's head.

8. To make the broom, tie straw to a twig with string.

Mrs. Snowman

1. Trace the pattern for the apron. Cut out the pattern and draw around it on felt. Cut out the felt apron.

   Cut a strip of felt that is about 12″ long and ½″ wide. Glue the strip over the top of the apron. Glue a piece of rickrack to the strip. When the glue is dry, tie the apron around Mrs. Snowman's waist.

2. Pull a piece of ribbon through the opening at the top of the jingle bell. Tie the ribbon around Mrs. Snowman's neck.

3. To make Mrs. Snowman's hat, draw around the saucer on felt. Cut out the felt circle. Put the juice can in the center of the circle and draw around the can. Cut out the circle. Place the hat on Mrs. Snowman's head. For a veil, put the hairnet over the hat.

Big Brother

1. Cut a strip of felt for a scarf. Tie the scarf around Brother's neck.

2. Wrap string around one of the baby socks, where the top of the sock meets the foot. Knot the string. Cut off the foot and throw it away.

Put the top of the sock on Brother's head. Turn up the edge. Glue strips of felt around the hat and glue a pom-pom on top.

Baby Sister

1. Cut a strip of felt for a scarf. Tie the scarf around Sister's neck.

2. Tie a piece of ribbon around one of the baby socks, where the top of the sock meets the foot. Cut off the foot and throw it away. Place the top of the sock on Sister's head. Turn up the edge twice so that the hat will fit.

3. Fold the square of white fabric in half, diagonally, to make a diaper. Pin the diaper on Sister.

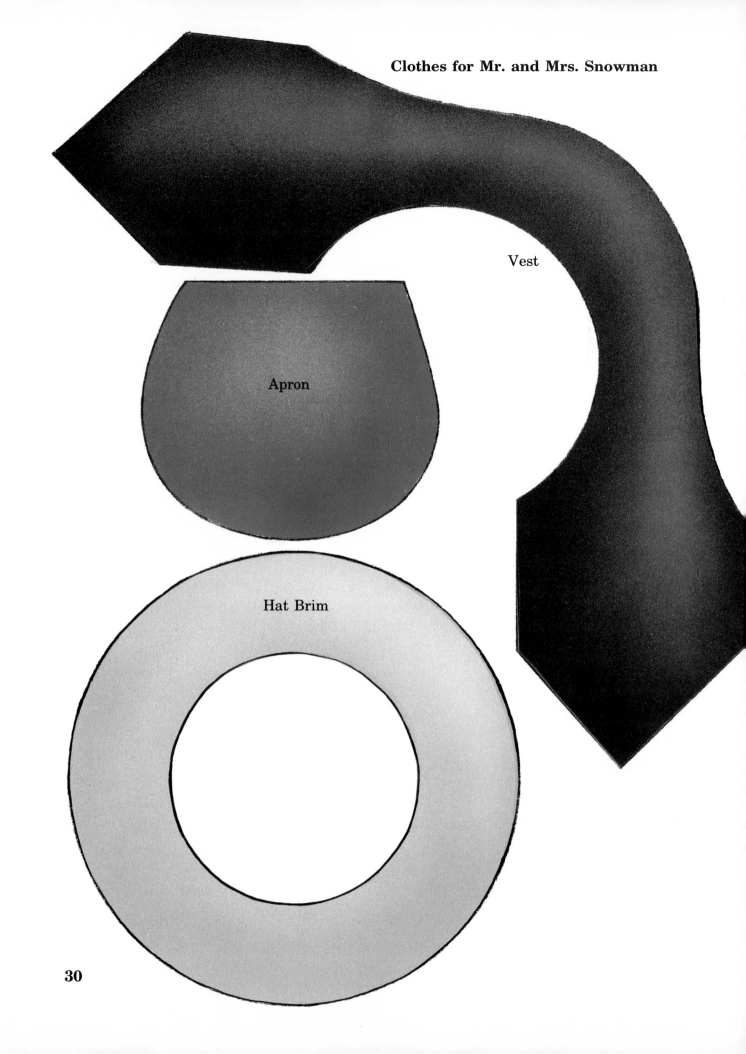

Vest

Apron

Hat Brim

Paper Penguins

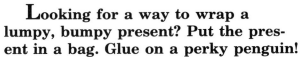
Looking for a way to wrap a lumpy, bumpy present? Put the present in a bag. Glue on a perky penguin!

You will need:
black fine-tip marker
tracing paper
scissors
construction paper in black, orange, white, red, and green
white glue
hole punch
gift bag
   (or wrapped present)

Level 2

1. Trace the pattern for the penguin. Cut out the pattern and draw around it on black paper. Cut out the black penguin.

2. Cut the beak and the feet from the penguin pattern. Draw around the beak and the feet on orange paper. Cut them out and glue them to the black penguin.

3. Cut the tummy from the penguin pattern. Draw around the tummy on white paper. Cut out the tummy and glue it on the black penguin.

4. Trace the patterns for the wing and the hat. Trace only the outline of the bow. Cut out the patterns. Draw around the wing on black paper, the hat on white paper, and the bow on red paper. Cut out the pieces and glue them on the black penguin.

5. Cut a red heart for the cheek. Cut a black strip and green holly leaves for trimming the hat. Punch red circles for berries and a white circle for the eye. Glue the pieces in place.

6. Draw a pupil on the penguin's eye. Draw lines on the bow (so it will look like a bow!), looking at the pattern to see how.

7. Glue the penguin onto the bag.

32

33

Cookie Cutter Cards

While your cookies are baking, use the cutters to make colorful cards. Here's how!

You will need:
construction paper
pencil
ruler
scissors
acrylic paint
paper plates
plastic cookie cutters
newspaper
paintbrush
white glue
ribbon bows

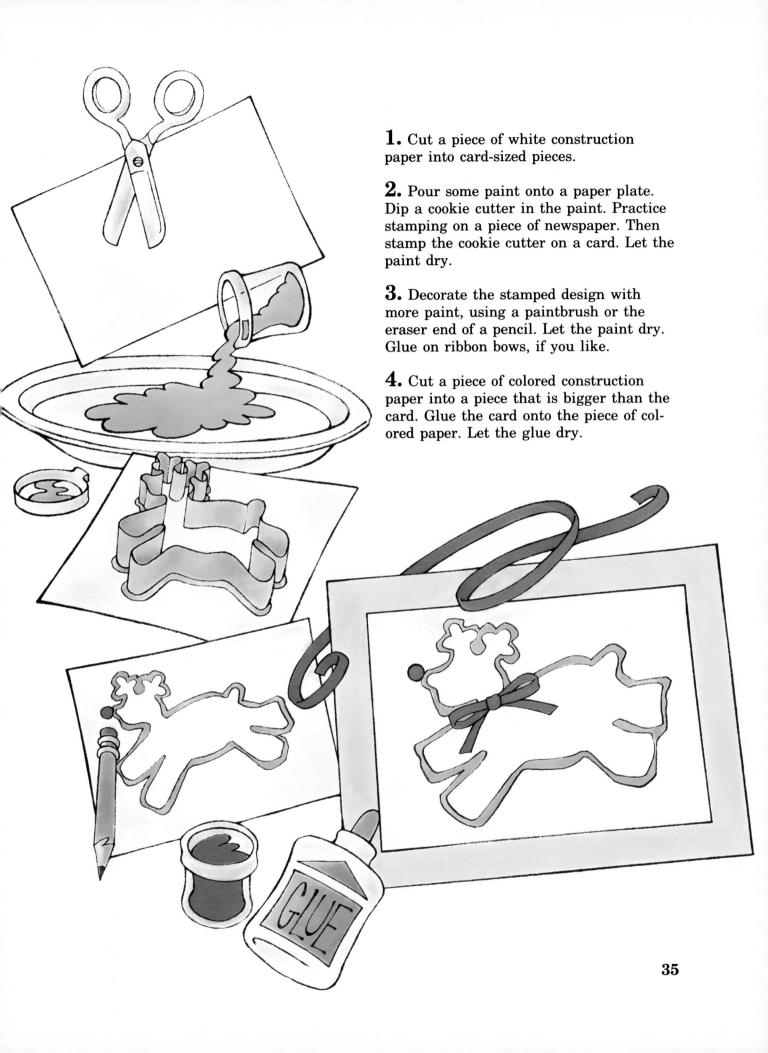

1. Cut a piece of white construction paper into card-sized pieces.

2. Pour some paint onto a paper plate. Dip a cookie cutter in the paint. Practice stamping on a piece of newspaper. Then stamp the cookie cutter on a card. Let the paint dry.

3. Decorate the stamped design with more paint, using a paintbrush or the eraser end of a pencil. Let the paint dry. Glue on ribbon bows, if you like.

4. Cut a piece of colored construction paper into a piece that is bigger than the card. Glue the card onto the piece of colored paper. Let the glue dry.

35

Cute'n Curly Santa Wrap

Ho, ho, ho! Won't Santa look jolly under somebody's tree!

You will need:
pencil
tracing paper
scissors
construction or wrapping paper in pink, white, red, and black
white glue
hole punch
heart sticker
wrapped present

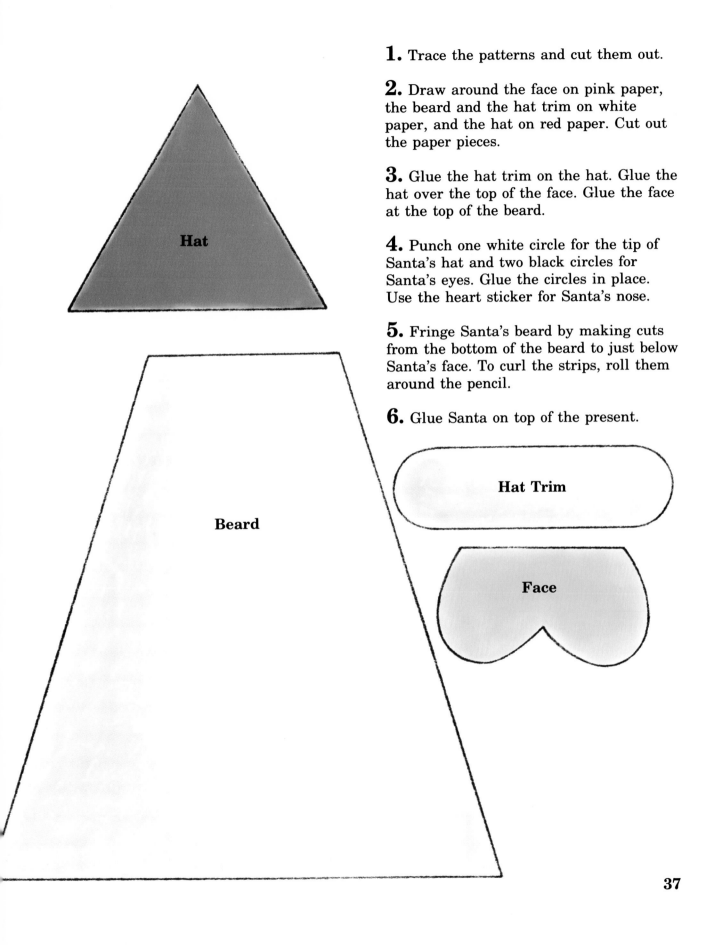

1. Trace the patterns and cut them out.

2. Draw around the face on pink paper, the beard and the hat trim on white paper, and the hat on red paper. Cut out the paper pieces.

3. Glue the hat trim on the hat. Glue the hat over the top of the face. Glue the face at the top of the beard.

4. Punch one white circle for the tip of Santa's hat and two black circles for Santa's eyes. Glue the circles in place. Use the heart sticker for Santa's nose.

5. Fringe Santa's beard by making cuts from the bottom of the beard to just below Santa's face. To curl the strips, roll them around the pencil.

6. Glue Santa on top of the present.

Hat

Beard

Hat Trim

Face

Scrappy Snowman Card

It takes a little of this and a little of that to make this cute card. Make a bunch. Send the cards to school friends. Send one to your teacher, too!

You will need:
construction paper
white glue
bag ties
heart stickers
tiny candies
scissors
scraps of Christmas paper and ribbon

1. Fold a sheet of construction paper in half to make a card.

2. Tear three circles for the snowman from white paper. Glue the circles on the card. Before the glue dries, glue bag ties for arms under the middle circle.

3. Tear paper to make a hat, a scarf, and mittens. Glue them in place.

4. Use heart stickers for eyes and a bag tie for a mouth. Glue on a little wad of paper for a nose. Glue on tiny candies for buttons.

5. Fold small pieces of paper and wrap them with Christmas paper to make presents. Tie ribbon around the presents. Glue them on the card.

39

Kitchen Cover-Up

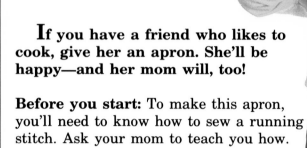

    If you have a friend who likes to cook, give her an apron. She'll be happy—and her mom will, too!

Before you start: To make this apron, you'll need to know how to sew a running stitch. Ask your mom to teach you how.

You will need:
pencil
yardstick
26″ x 27″ piece of Christmas fabric
scissors
4⅓ yards of bias tape (double-fold)
straight pins
embroidery thread
needle with large eye

40

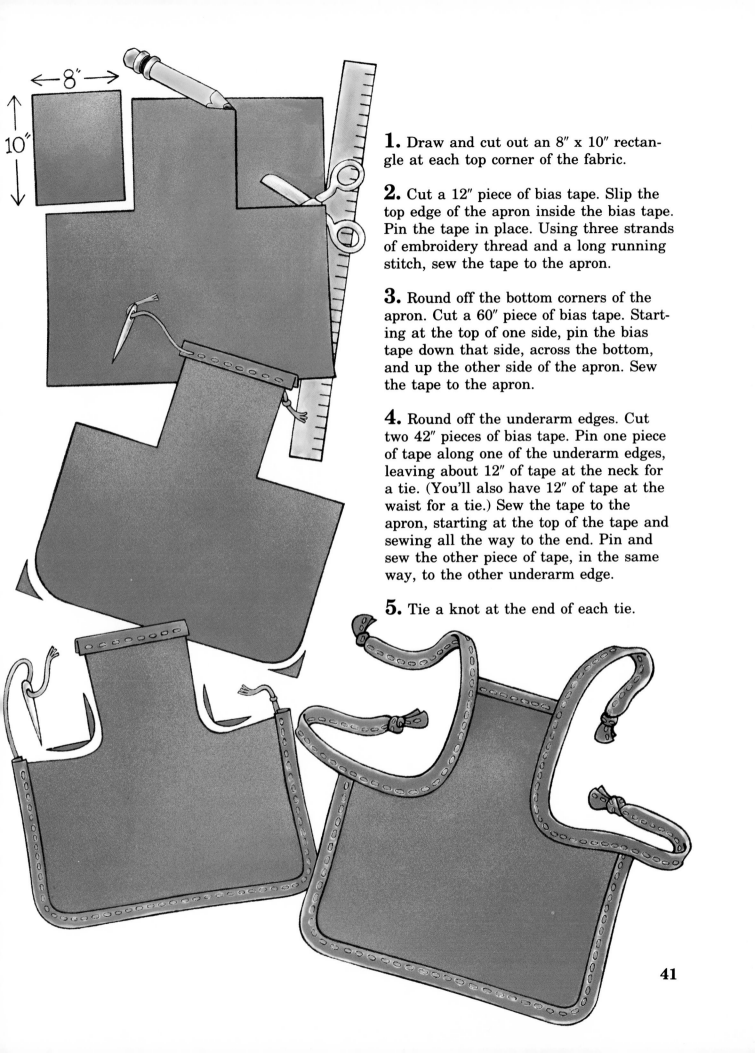

1. Draw and cut out an 8″ x 10″ rectangle at each top corner of the fabric.

2. Cut a 12″ piece of bias tape. Slip the top edge of the apron inside the bias tape. Pin the tape in place. Using three strands of embroidery thread and a long running stitch, sew the tape to the apron.

3. Round off the bottom corners of the apron. Cut a 60″ piece of bias tape. Starting at the top of one side, pin the bias tape down that side, across the bottom, and up the other side of the apron. Sew the tape to the apron.

4. Round off the underarm edges. Cut two 42″ pieces of bias tape. Pin one piece of tape along one of the underarm edges, leaving about 12″ of tape at the neck for a tie. (You'll also have 12″ of tape at the waist for a tie.) Sew the tape to the apron, starting at the top of the tape and sewing all the way to the end. Pin and sew the other piece of tape, in the same way, to the other underarm edge.

5. Tie a knot at the end of each tie.

Busy Books

Want to give your parents an extra-special present? What could be nicer than a helping hand!

You will need (for each book):
4 (3″ x 6″) pieces wrapping paper
2 (3″ x 6″) pieces cardboard
glue stick
3″ square of green construction paper
scissors
fine-tip markers
scrap of white paper
heart or star sticker
4 (4″ x 7″) pieces clear contact paper
ruler
hole punch
9″ x 12″ piece of construction paper
broad-tip marker
½ yard of ribbon or 2 paper fasteners

1. Glue the pieces of wrapping paper to the pieces of cardboard. Use these for the front and back covers.

2. Fold the 3″ square of green construction paper in half. Starting at the top of the fold, cut out half a tree. Open the tree and cut along the fold. Glue the tree to the cover, leaving a space between the halves.

3. Using a fine-tip marker and writing small, write MOTHER'S or FATHER'S and JOB COUPON BOOK on a piece of white paper. Cut out the words and glue them on the tree. Add a heart or star sticker or other decorations, if you like.

4. Put a piece of contact paper face-down on the table and peel off the backing. Center the front cover on top of the contact paper and press. Cut off the edges of the contact paper. Cover the other side of the front cover the same way. Then cover both sides of the back cover.

5. Punch two holes, one below the other, at the left end of the front cover. Put the front cover on top of the back cover and mark the holes. Punch holes in the marks on the back cover.

6. To make the coupons, fold the 9″ x 12″ piece of construction paper from left to right so that the short ends meet. Measure 3″ from the top and draw a line from side to side. Draw another line 3″ below the first one. Cut along the lines.

7. Draw a dotted line down the middle of each coupon. Using a fine-tip marker, write TEAR ALONG DOTTED LINE to the left of the line. Using the broad-tip marker, write the job title to the right of the line.

8. Stack the folded coupons inside each other. Using one of the covers as a guide, punch holes in the coupons.

9. Place the coupons between the covers. Use ribbon or paper fasteners to hold the covers and coupons together.

Clown Bulletin Board

A bulletin board is fun to have and handy, too. Bet you know someone who could use one of these!

You will need:
piece of plastic foam (1″ thick)
yardstick
piece of felt for covering the plastic foam
pencil
scissors
white glue
pushpins
tracing paper
scraps of felt for the clown
ribbon for the clown's bow
bag tie
ribbon (1″ wide) for trim

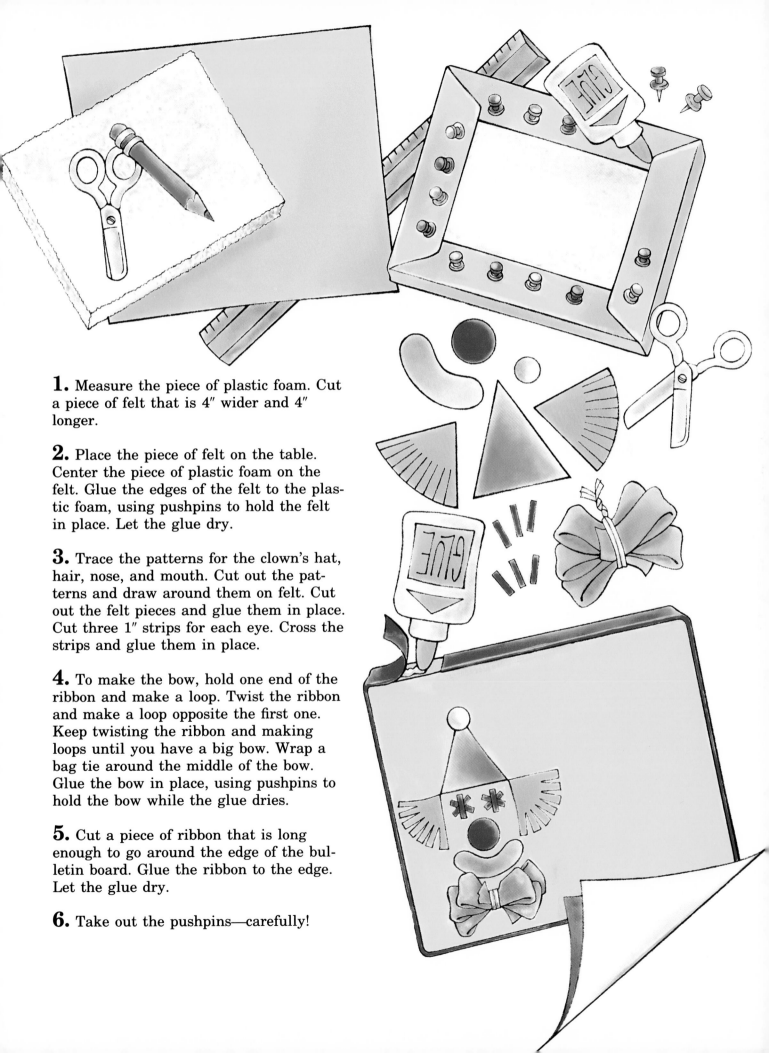

1. Measure the piece of plastic foam. Cut a piece of felt that is 4″ wider and 4″ longer.

2. Place the piece of felt on the table. Center the piece of plastic foam on the felt. Glue the edges of the felt to the plastic foam, using pushpins to hold the felt in place. Let the glue dry.

3. Trace the patterns for the clown's hat, hair, nose, and mouth. Cut out the patterns and draw around them on felt. Cut out the felt pieces and glue them in place. Cut three 1″ strips for each eye. Cross the strips and glue them in place.

4. To make the bow, hold one end of the ribbon and make a loop. Twist the ribbon and make a loop opposite the first one. Keep twisting the ribbon and making loops until you have a big bow. Wrap a bag tie around the middle of the bow. Glue the bow in place, using pushpins to hold the bow while the glue dries.

5. Cut a piece of ribbon that is long enough to go around the edge of the bulletin board. Glue the ribbon to the edge. Let the glue dry.

6. Take out the pushpins—carefully!

Patterns for Clown

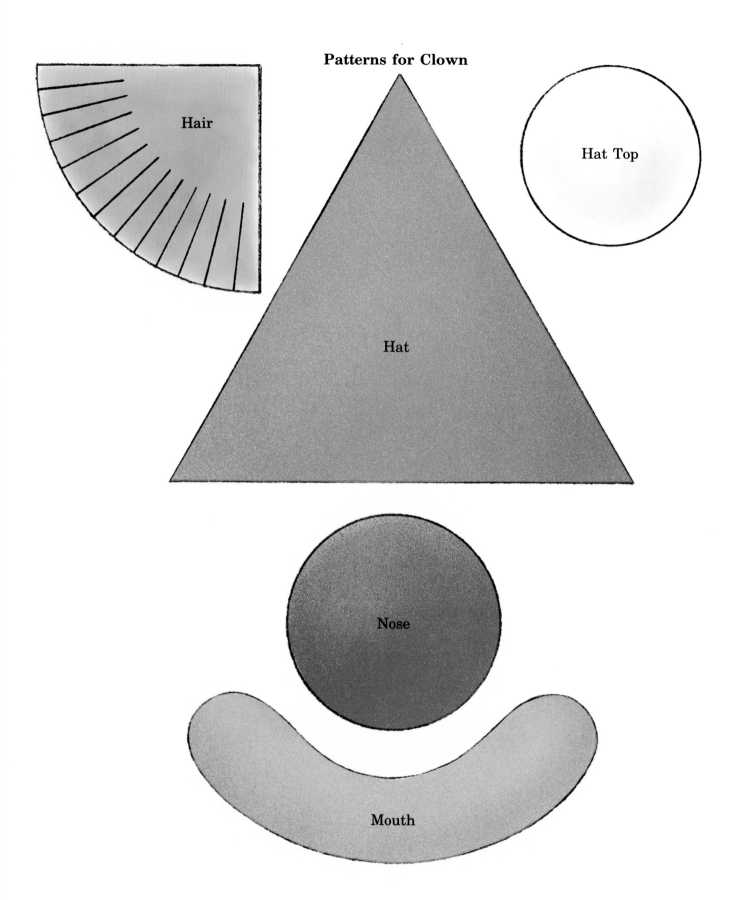

Hair

Hat

Hat Top

Nose

Mouth

46

Jiffy Jewelry

Making paper jewelry is not only quick but easy, too. Start with these shapes. Then have some fun designing your own!

You will need:

construction paper
scissors
pencil
poster paper
pushpin
Mod Podge
saucer

paper towels
paintbrush
pair of ear posts
pin back
stapler
1 yard of narrow
  ribbon

Level 2

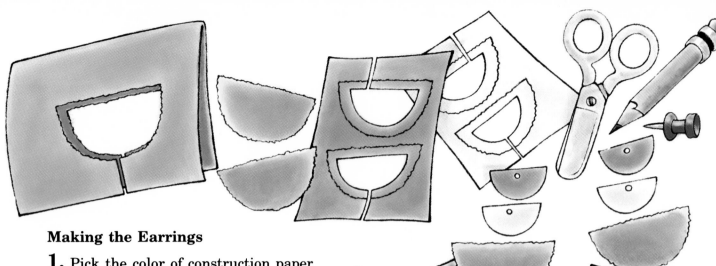

Making the Earrings

1. Pick the color of construction paper that you want to use for the basic shape of the earrings. Fold the piece of paper in half. Tear or cut out a shape that you like for the earrings.

2. For the backings, draw around each earring (you'll have two because you folded the paper) on the same color of construction paper. Then draw around the earrings on poster paper. Cut out the four backings, cutting inside the outline so that the backings will be smaller than the earrings.

3. Match up the backings for each earring. In the center of the top third of each set of backings, make a hole for the ear post with a pushpin.

4. Pick the colors of paper that you want to use for the decorative shapes. Fold the pieces of paper in half. Tear or cut out the decorative shapes.

5. Put some Mod Podge in the saucer. Put the earrings on a paper towel and paint the front of them with Mod Podge. While the earrings are still wet, add a decorative shape to each. Apply another coat of Mod Podge. Keep adding decorative shapes and applying Mod Podge until you like the look of the earrings. Let the Mod Podge dry—thoroughly.

6. Push a poster-paper backing onto each ear post. Brush the backings with Mod Podge. Push the construction-paper back-

ings onto the posts and brush the backings with Mod Podge. Let the Mod Podge dry.

7. Turn over the earring and paint the back with Mod Podge. Apply the backings. Paint the back of the backings with Mod Podge. Let the Mod Podge dry.

48

Making the Pin and Necklace

1. To make a pin or necklace, tear or cut out the basic shape from construction paper.

2. For the backings, draw around the basic shape on construction paper and poster paper. Cut out the backings, cutting inside the outline.

3. Tear or cut out the decorative shapes. Using Mod Podge, apply the decorative shapes to the basic shape. Let the Mod Podge dry.

4. To finish the pin, turn the basic shape over. Use Mod Podge to apply the poster-paper backing, the construction-paper backing, and the pin back. Let the Mod Podge dry.

5. To finish the necklace, cut the ribbon in half. Staple one end of each ribbon to the poster-paper backing. Apply the poster-paper backing and the construction-paper backing to the back of the basic shape, using Mod Podge. Let the Mod Podge dry.

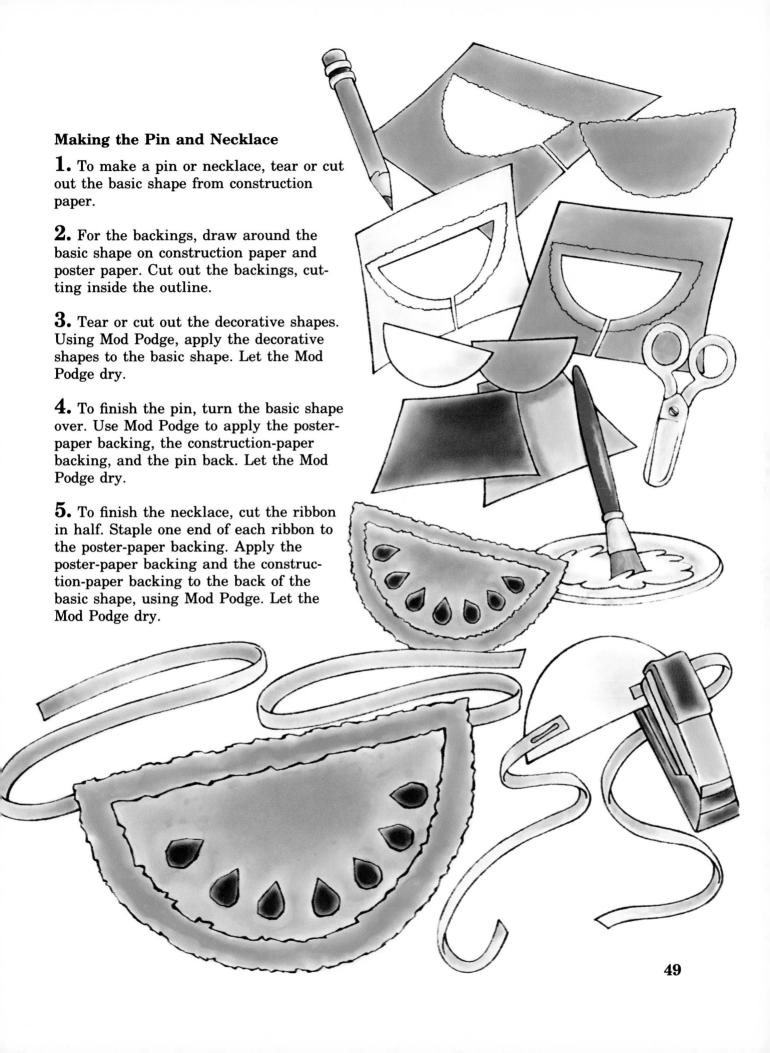

Coupon Catcher

Whoever gets this present will love you, too!

You will need:
5″ x 12″ piece of felt
ruler
white glue
6″ piece of eyelet trim
6″ piece of ribbon
pencil
tracing paper
scrap of felt for heart
Alpha-Bits
magnetic tape

1. Fold up the piece of felt about 3″ from the bottom. Glue the side edges together to make a little pocket.

2. Glue the piece of eyelet across the top of the pocket, wrapping the ends to the back. Glue the piece of ribbon on top of the eyelet.

3. Trace and cut out the pattern for the heart. Draw around the heart on the scrap of felt. Cut out the felt heart and glue it in place. Spell I LOVE YOU with Alpha-Bits. Glue the letters across the heart. Let the glue dry.

4. Cut a strip of magnetic tape and stick it on the back.

Leather-Look Desk Set

Surprise your brother or best buddy with a desk set. See if he can guess what materials you used!

You will need:
masking tape
12-ounce juice can
rag
brown shoe polish (paste)
cigar box
pencil
felt
scissors
glue stick
old picture frame
picture

Pencil Holder

1. Wrap strips of masking tape around the top and the bottom of the can so that the edges of the tape line up with the edges of the can. Cover the rest of the can with strips of tape.

2. Tear off pieces of tape in different shapes and sizes and stick them all over the can. Keep adding pieces of tape until you can't see the design on the can.

3. Using the rag, rub shoe polish on the can. Let the shoe polish dry.

Picture Frame

1. Slide the back from the picture frame and carefully remove the piece of glass. Set these aside.

2. Cover the frame with strips of tape, using a pencil if you need to, to poke the tape in place (inside the sides). Cover the strips of tape with pieces of tape.

3. Rub shoe polish on the frame. Let the shoe polish dry.

4. Put a picture in the frame. Put the frame back together.

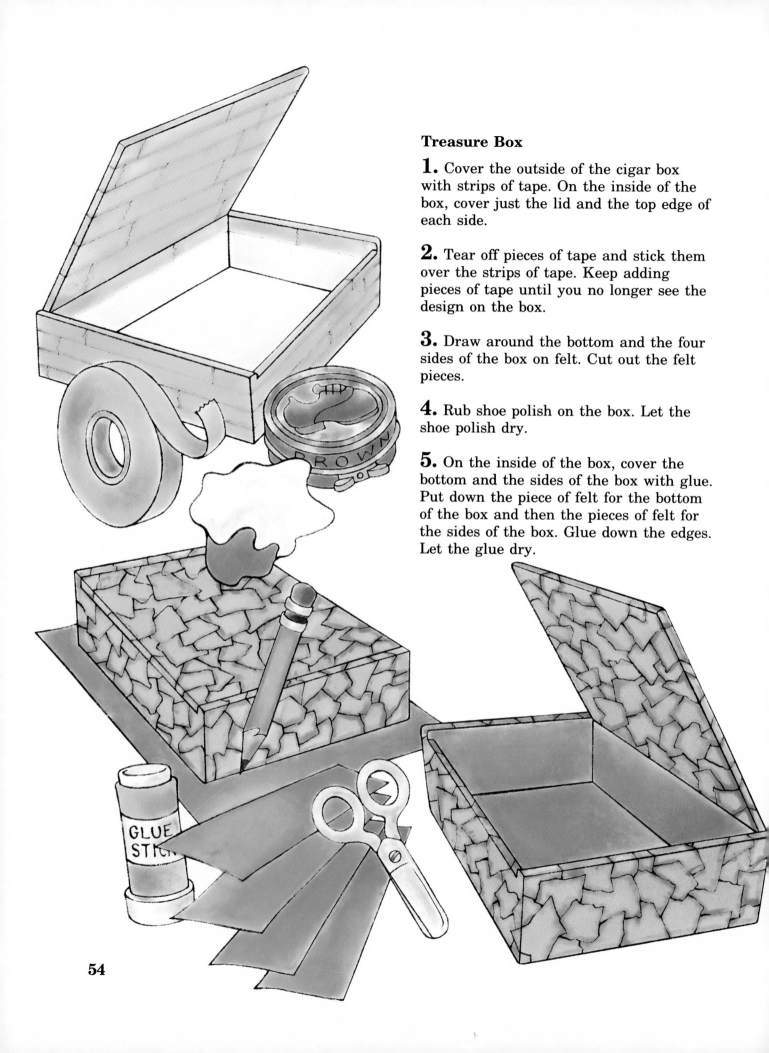

Treasure Box

1. Cover the outside of the cigar box with strips of tape. On the inside of the box, cover just the lid and the top edge of each side.

2. Tear off pieces of tape and stick them over the strips of tape. Keep adding pieces of tape until you no longer see the design on the box.

3. Draw around the bottom and the four sides of the box on felt. Cut out the felt pieces.

4. Rub shoe polish on the box. Let the shoe polish dry.

5. On the inside of the box, cover the bottom and the sides of the box with glue. Put down the piece of felt for the bottom of the box and then the pieces of felt for the sides of the box. Glue down the edges. Let the glue dry.

54

A Pudgy Pair

Stitch and stuff socks to make these plump snowmen. They're very soft and snuggly, too!

Before you start: You can either color or embroider the face on the doll. To embroider the face, you'll need to know how to satin-stitch and backstitch. Ask your mom to teach you how.

You will need:
18″-long white tube sock (size 10-13)
ruler
pencil
scissors
sewing needle and thread
polyester stuffing
string
fine-tip markers or embroidery
   needle and thread
ribbon
scraps of red and green felt
white glue

Level 3

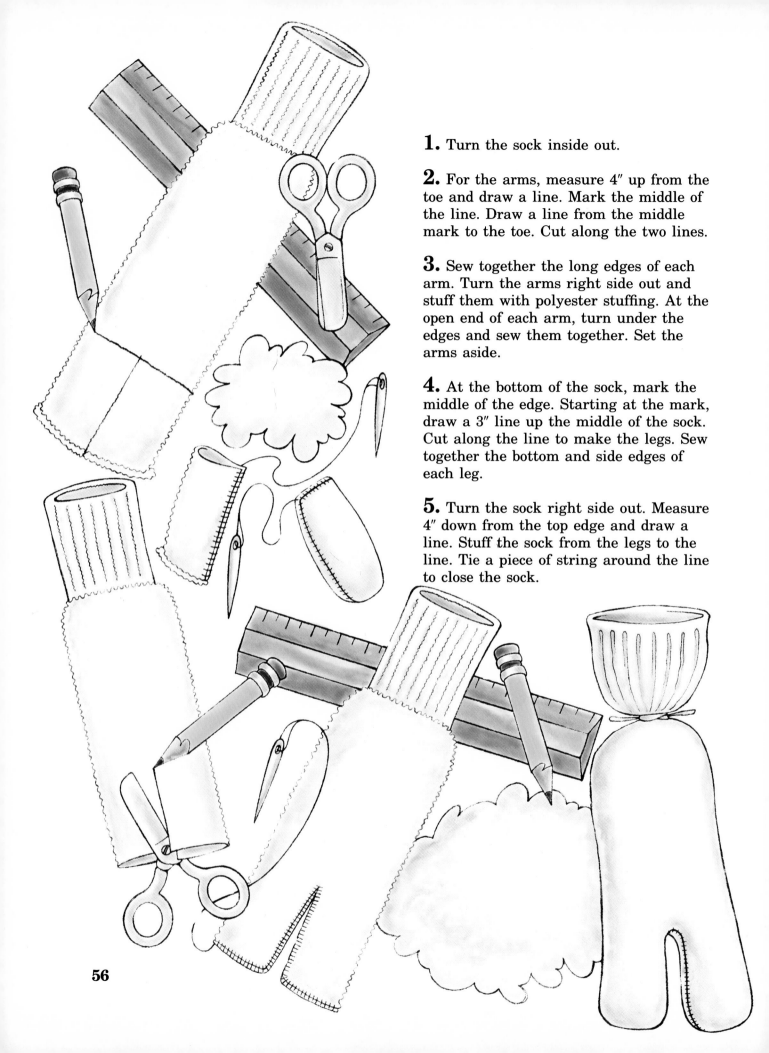

1. Turn the sock inside out.

2. For the arms, measure 4″ up from the toe and draw a line. Mark the middle of the line. Draw a line from the middle mark to the toe. Cut along the two lines.

3. Sew together the long edges of each arm. Turn the arms right side out and stuff them with polyester stuffing. At the open end of each arm, turn under the edges and sew them together. Set the arms aside.

4. At the bottom of the sock, mark the middle of the edge. Starting at the mark, draw a 3″ line up the middle of the sock. Cut along the line to make the legs. Sew together the bottom and side edges of each leg.

5. Turn the sock right side out. Measure 4″ down from the top edge and draw a line. Stuff the sock from the legs to the line. Tie a piece of string around the line to close the sock.

6. To make the doll's head, tie another piece of string 3″ below the first one.

7. Using the pencil, draw eyes, eyebrows, a nose, and a mouth. Color the features, or embroider them, using satin stitch for the eyes and nose and backstitch for the eyebrows and mouth.

8. Sew the arms to the body, just below the neck. Tie a ribbon around the neck and make a bow.

9. Turn the top of the sock down on top of the head to make the hat. Turn up the edges to make a cuff. Cut holly leaves and berries from felt and glue them on the cuff. Let the glue dry.

PARENTS' WORKSHOP
Great Gifts for Children

Sitting Ducks

Sized just right for little folks, this stool is made for stepping up—oops, or sitting down—depending on the nature of the business at hand.

You will need:
brown paper for pattern
yardstick
1 (4′) 1 x 12
2 (8″) 1 x 1s
electric band or saber saw
sandpaper
16 (1¼″) finishing nails
#1 nail set
electric drill with countersink and ⅛″ bits
4 (1¼″) #6 wood screws
wood filler
enamel undercoat
paintbrushes
high-gloss enamel paint (white, orange,
    yellow, and black)
1½ yards (1⅜″-wide) ribbon

Note: The smooth side of the ducks should face out and the smooth side of the seat should face up. Countersink all nails, using the nail set; countersink all screws, using the countersink bit to drill a hole for the screw head and the ⅛″ bit to drill a hole for the screw shaft.

1. Enlarge pattern for duck to full size. Cut out the pattern. Mark the front A and the back B.

2. On the rough side of the 1 x 12, draw around side A of the duck, then side B, for the ends of the stool. Draw an 8″ x 11″ rectangle for the step (seat). Using the saw, cut out the ducks and the step. Sand the edges and sides of all the wood pieces, including the 1 x 1s.

3. On the rough side of one duck, measure 5½″ from the base (bottom of feet) and draw a line across the duck parallel to the base. Center the top edge of one 1 x 1 on the line. Attach the 1 x 1 to the duck with two finishing nails, inserting the nails from the outside of the duck into the 1 x 1. Secure each end of the 1 x

1 with a wood screw, drilling the holes and inserting the screws from the outside of the duck into the 1 x 1. Attach other 1 x 1 to other duck in the same way.

4. Attach the step to the 1 x 1s with six nails (three at each end of the step), inserting the nails from the top of the step into the 1 x 1s. To secure the step, attach the ducks to the ends of the step, using three nails at each end.

5. Use wood filler to fill all holes and let dry; sand to smooth. Apply enamel undercoat to entire stool and let dry.

6. Paint the entire stool white, applying two to three coats and allowing the paint to dry after each application. On both sides of the ducks, paint the feet orange, the bill yellow, and the eyes black. Let the paint dry.

7. Cut the ribbon in half. Tie a ribbon around each duck's neck and make a bow.

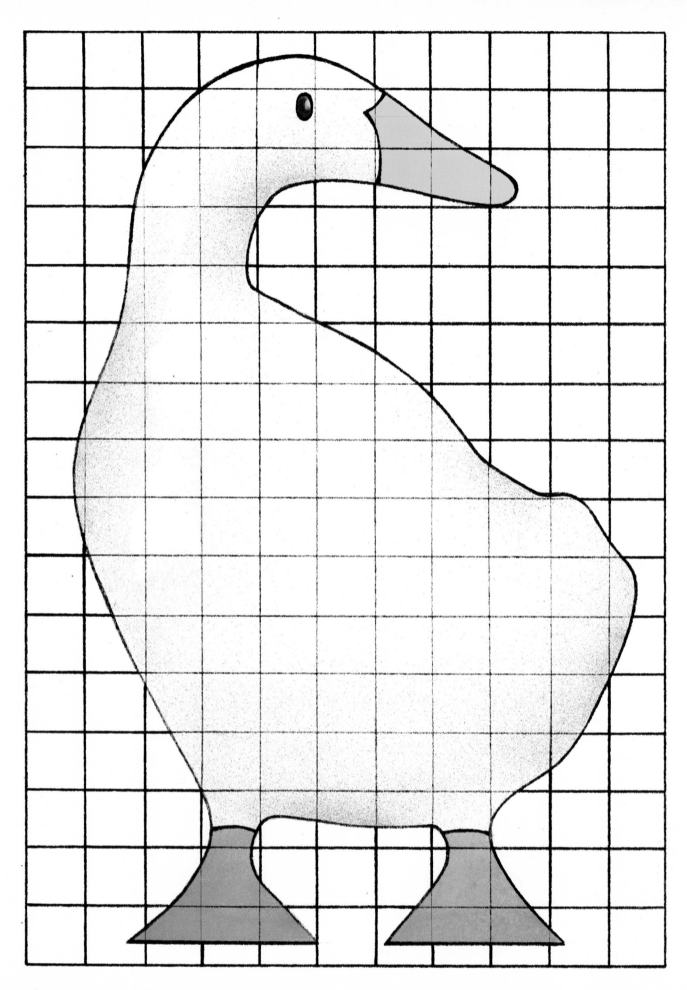

One square = 1″.

Tabletop Tunes

Pink paint and a polka-dotted bow add a colorful touch to this tiny elephant, who does more, by the way, than stand around and steal hearts. Wind him up, and he'll croon a tune that will add sunshine to a dreary day or sweeten dreams at night.

You will need:
tracing paper
7½″ x 12″ (¼″) plywood
small music box (2″ x 2″ x 1⅛″) with key
  that unscrews
ruler
scroll saw
electric drill and ⅜″ bit
sandpaper
acrylic paint (white, black, and red)
paintbrushes
carbon paper
epoxy glue
toothpick
⅓ yard (⅝″-wide) ribbon
white glue

1. Trace the pattern for the elephant (including features) onto tracing paper. Cut out the pattern. Mark the front A and the back B.

On the rough side of the plywood, draw around side A for the front elephant. For the back elephant, draw around side B.

Unscrew key from the music box. On rough side of the back elephant, center the music box and draw around it. Measure placement of keyhole on music box and mark placement on back elephant.

2. Cut out the elephants with the scroll saw. (To facilitate cutting around the elephant's ears, enter the V area from one direction, back the saw out, and reenter the area from the opposite direction as shown.) Using the drill and the ⅜" bit, drill keyhole in back elephant as marked. Sand entire surface of both elephants, sanding with the grain.

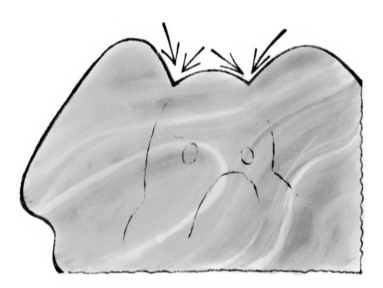

3. Mix white paint with a small amount of black paint to make light gray. Paint sides and edges of both elephants. Allow the paint to dry. Apply three or four more coats of paint, letting the paint dry after each application.

4. Using carbon paper and a pencil, transfer features (face, ears, trunk, and hearts) to the front elephant; reverse the pattern and transfer ears only to the back elephant.

Mix a small amount of red and white paint to make pink. Paint the hearts and let dry. Repeat until pink covers gray.

Using the black paint, paint the edges of the elephants. On the front elephant, outline the features and the outer edges; paint two dots for eyes. On the back elephant, outline the ears and the outer edges; paint a tail. Allow the paint to dry.

5. To roughen surface, sand the front and back of the music box. On the rough side of the back elephant, position the music box so that keyholes line up. Draw around the music box to mark placement on the elephant. Using a toothpick, spread epoxy glue within the marked area and on the back of the music box; glue the elephant and music box together. Place a book on top of the music box to apply pressure while the glue dries.

When the glue is dry, place the front elephant (rough side) on the music box, aligning the edges of the front and back elephants. Mark placement of the music box on the front elephant; glue the two together, spreading glue inside the marked area and on the front of the music box. Apply pressure while the glue dries.

6. Tie the ribbon into a bow and attach it with white glue to the front elephant. Let the glue dry. Replace the key.

Sunbonnet Sheep

Sweet Sue, how do you do? A wee shy, but smart in her snappy straw hat, this lamb will be the darling of any little girl.

You will need:

tracing paper
3 yards (45″-wide) white cotton fabric
¼ yard (60″-wide) black velveteen
thread to match
7″ x 11″ piece of pink lining for ears
scrap of black lining for eyelids
water-soluble marking pen
polyester stuffing
black heavy-duty thread

2 (⅝″) buttons for eyes
1 (⅝″) black button for nose
compass
1¼ yards (⅜″-wide) pink ribbon
doll's (4½″-diameter) straw hat
tiny imitation flowers
pink feather
black elastic thread
1 yard (⅞″-wide) pink ribbon

1. Trace and cut out the patterns, adding ¼″ seam allowances. Transfer patterns to fabrics and cut as marked. Using the water-soluble pen, transfer markings.

2. Pin the body pieces with right sides together. Sew, leaving 2″ opening for turning as marked. Turn body right side out; press. Stuff with polyester stuffing and slip-stitch opening closed.

3. Pin the leg pieces in pairs with right sides together. Sew, leaving top open as marked. Turn legs; fold down raw edges ¼″ and stuff legs firmly. With side seams facing out, sew the legs to the body as marked, using heavy-duty thread.

4. Sew buttons for eyes to head pieces as marked. Pin the head pieces with right sides together and sew, leaving neck open. Turn; fold under raw edge ½″ and stuff head. Using heavy-duty thread, sew the head to the body as marked; sew on button for nose.

Pin lining to eyelids with right sides together and sew, leaving straight edge open. Turn; fold under raw edges ¼″ and slip-stitch openings closed. Sew eyelids to head, stitching around curved edge only and leaving button eyes partially exposed.

Pin lining to ears with right sides together and sew, leaving top edge open as marked. Turn ears; fold under raw edges ¼″ and slip-stitch opening closed. Fold under top corners of each ear as marked and tack the corners in place. Sew the ears to the head as marked.

5. Fold the remaining white fabric with selvage ends together. Using the compass, draw fifty-five circles, each with a 5″ diameter, on the fabric. Cut out the circles. (You'll have 110 circles, which should be enough to cover the sheep's body. However, the number needed can vary, depending on how firmly the circles are stuffed.)

To stuff each circle, fold under the raw edge ¼″ and sew with a basting stitch. Pull thread to partially gather. Lightly stuff the circle and gather again, leaving ½″ opening; backstitch.

Sew eight of the circles around sheep's neck, placing circles so that they cover the neck seam. Sew remaining circles to rest of body. When finished, tack bottom corners of front legs together, at side seams; tack back legs in same way.

6. Cut a 19″ piece of the ⅜″-wide ribbon. Wrap the ribbon around the crown of the hat, overlapping the ribbon ends at the back. Sew the ribbons, where they cross, to the hat; tack the flowers over the stitches.

From the ⅜″-wide ribbon, cut a 22″ piece. Make four 2″ loops with the piece of ribbon. Sew through the center of the loops and then sew the looped ribbon over the flowers. Sew the feather to the hat.

Cut a piece of black elastic thread that will be long enough to hold the hat on the sheep's head; tack the ends of the elastic to the inside of the hat. Place the hat on the sheep's head. Tie the ⅞″-wide ribbon around the sheep's neck and make a bow.

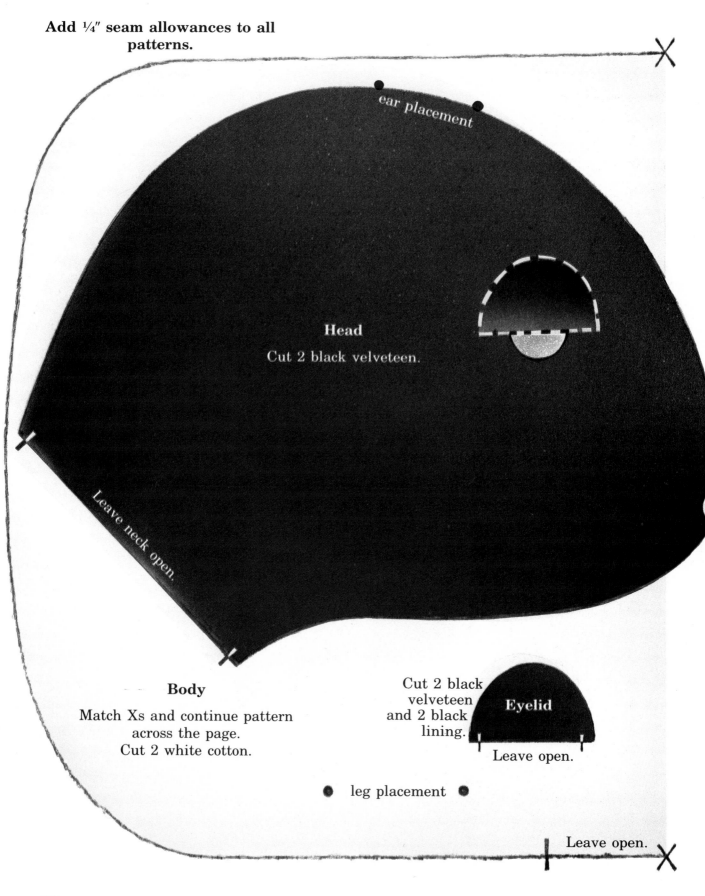

Add ¼″ seam allowances to all patterns.

ear placement

Head

Cut 2 black velveteen.

Leave neck open.

Body

Match Xs and continue pattern across the page.
Cut 2 white cotton.

Cut 2 black velveteen and 2 black lining.

Eyelid

Leave open.

leg placement

Leave open.

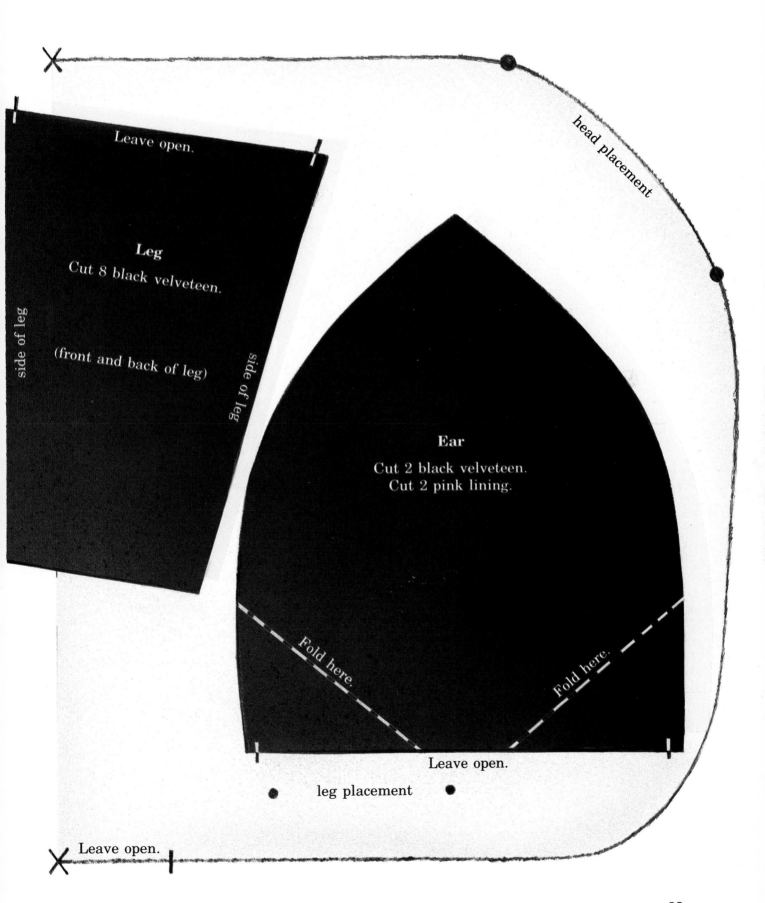

Leave open.

Leg
Cut 8 black velveteen.

(front and back of leg)

side of leg

side of leg

head placement

Ear
Cut 2 black velveteen.
Cut 2 pink lining.

Fold here.

Fold here.

Leave open.

leg placement

Leave open.

69

Bear Chair

What's cute and holds kids, plus kids' coats, hats, books, and other belongings? This bear chair. Talk about a good seat—it must be the best in the house!

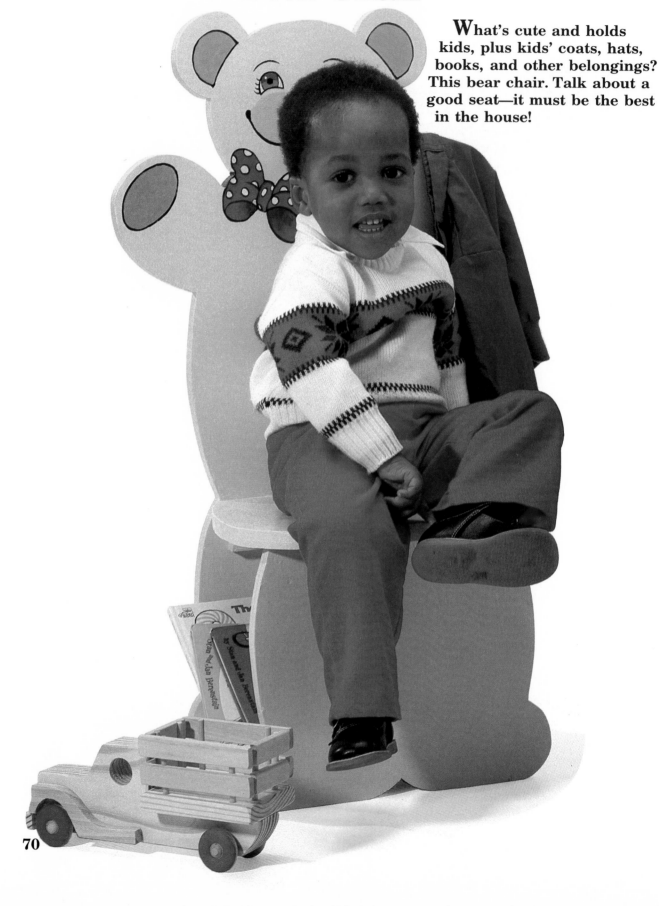

You will need:

brown paper for pattern
T square
3' x 4' (¾") best-grade
  plywood
electric saber saw
1 (10") 1 x 2 for seat
  support
18 (1½") #8 wood screws
electric drill with countersink
  and ⅛" bits
2 (8¼") 1 x 2s for shelf supports
sandpaper
wood filler
enamel undercoat
paintbrushes
high-gloss enamel paint

Note: Countersink all screws, using the countersink bit to drill a hole for the screw head and the ⅛" bit to drill a hole for the screw shaft.

1. Enlarge patterns for chair back (includes back legs), front legs, and seat on brown paper. Cut out the patterns.

2. Lay the patterns face down on the rough side of the ¾" plywood, placing the patterns so that the bottom of the front and back legs and the back edge of the seat are on the straight (factory) edge of the plywood. Draw around the patterns. Draw an 8¼" x 11½" rectangle for the shelf. Carefully cut out the four pieces of wood, using the saber saw.

3. Lay the chair back, smooth side up, on the floor. Align the front legs, smooth side up, with the back legs and draw a line across the back of the chair, along the top edge of the front legs. Center the seat support (10"-long 1 x 2) along the line so that one 2" side lies below the line, flat against the chair back. Attach the support to the chair back with three wood

screws, drilling the holes and inserting the screws through the support into the back.

4. Stand the shelf supports (8¼"-long 1 x 2s) on 1" sides. Place the shelf on top of the supports with edges flush. Attach the shelf to the supports with four screws (two on each side), drilling the holes and inserting the screws through the top of the shelf into the supports.

5. Align the bottom of the front legs, with right side facing out, with the bottom of the shelf supports; center the shelf. Secure the front legs to the shelf with three wood screws, drilling the holes and inserting the screws through the legs into the shelf. With wrong side facing out and with edges of front and back legs aligned, attach the back of the chair to the shelf in the same way.

6. Rest the seat, with curved edge out, on the seat support and front legs. Attach the seat to the support with two screws, drilling holes and inserting the screws through the top of the seat into each end of the support. With front legs parallel to chair back, attach the seat to the front legs with three wood screws, drilling the holes and inserting the screws through top of seat into top of legs.

7. Sand all rough surfaces. Fill holes with wood filler; let dry and sand again. Apply enamel undercoat and let dry; sand lightly.

8. Paint chair desired color, applying several coats of paint and letting the paint dry after each application. Draw bear's features on the chair, using the photograph and pattern as a guide. Paint the features. Allow paint to dry.

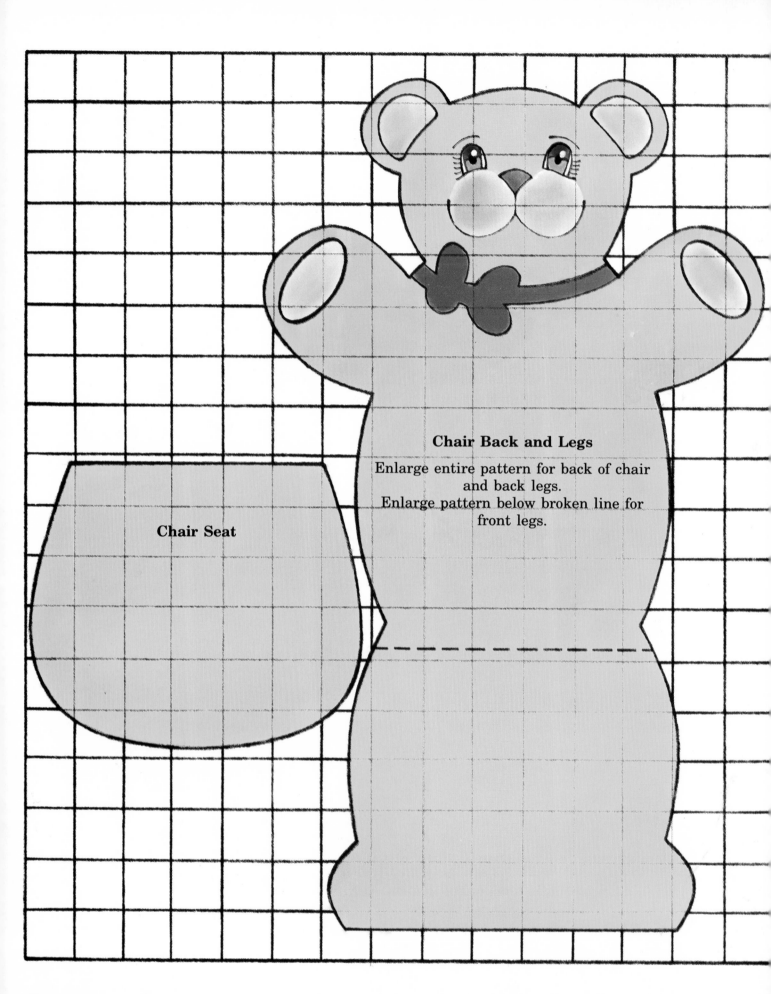

Chair Seat

Chair Back and Legs

Enlarge entire pattern for back of chair
and back legs.
Enlarge pattern below broken line for
front legs.

One square = 2″.

PJ Hideaway

Not one to go unnoticed, this lion is loaded with lovable good looks. Although designed as a pajama guard, he's perfectly content to be idle. Stuffed, he'll sit on a bed or shelf, ready and waiting for kisses, hugs, or a pat on the back.

A beauty to behold, this creature is, however, a bit beastly to make, unless you're an experienced sewer. In this case, allow ample time, follow the steps carefully, and enjoy the challenge and the ingenuity of the project.

You will need:

2 yards (45"-wide) light rust fabric
¼ yard (45"-wide) medium rust fabric
½ yard (45"-wide) dark rust fabric
⅓ yard (45"-wide) fabric for bow tie
thread to match
ruler (18" clear with ⅛" grid is helpful)
tape measure
scrap of fleece or batting (for ears)
scrap of fusible web (for heart cheeks)
water-soluble marking pen
tracing paper
rust embroidery floss
craft needles (sizes 2" and 3½" to 4")
polyester stuffing
2 (⅜") black shank buttons
quilting thread
thimble
⅔ yard (⅝"-wide) rust ribbon
light rust seam binding
12" light rust zipper

Cutting the Pieces

1. From light rust fabric, cut one 25¼" x 45" rectangle for body A (legs, outer mane, and body) and one 25¼" x 45" rectangle for body B (outer mane, head cover, and lining); cut one 6" x 24" rectangle for tail. From medium rust fabric, cut one 9" x 45" rectangle for inner mane. From dark rust fabric, cut one 4½" x 6" rectangle for tail and two 6½" x 45" rectangles for outer mane. Using water-soluble pen, transfer all pattern markings to wrong side of body A; transfer mane line and center front line to body B. (Figure A.)

2. Transfer patterns for face, back of head, cheek, and ear to fabrics and cut as marked. Transfer markings to right side of fabric pieces.

Sewing the Pieces

Note: Use ¼" seam allowance throughout unless instructed otherwise. Where gath-

ering is required, instructions call for machine basting. Use the 2" needle when sewing by hand except when sewing on the button eyes.

Head

1. Iron cheeks to sides of face with fusible web. Using buttonhole stitch and two strands of embroidery floss, sew cheeks to sides of face.

2. For each ear, place dark rust ear and light rust ear, right sides together, on top of fleece ear; sew three ears together, leaving bottom open. Grade seam allowances and clip curves. Turn ear right side out and press. Baste small pleat in dark rust ear as marked. Baste raw edge of ear to side of face, as marked, with dark rust ear facing right side of face.

3. With right sides together, sew face at center front; sew back of head at center back. Sew face to back of head, right sides together, leaving bottom open. Stitch head seams again to reinforce. Clip curves and turn head. Stuff head extra-firmly with polyester stuffing.

Using four strands of thread, hand-sew gathering stitches around base of neck, ¼" from raw edge. Pull threads to gather tightly; tie off.

4. To sew on buttons for eyes, use the 4" needle and four strands of thread. Insert needle in back of head, come up through front, catch button, and push needle back through head. Pull ends of thread tightly and tie together in back; knot. (Knots will not show since back of head will later be covered by lining.)

5. Using two strands of embroidery floss, outline-stitch eyebrows and mouth as marked; satin-stitch nose. Set head aside.

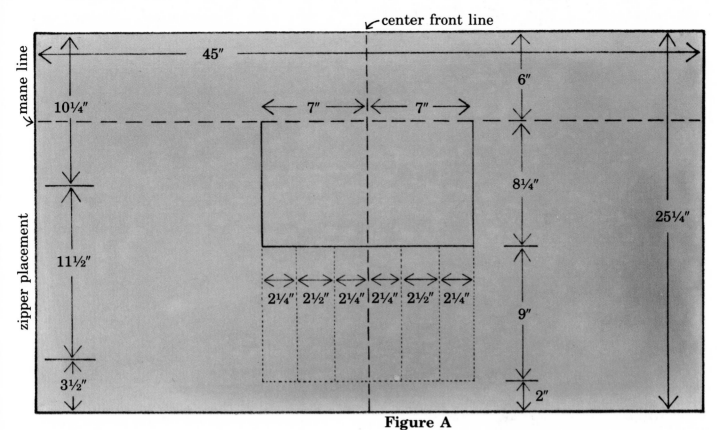

center front line

mane line

zipper placement

45"

10¼"

11½"

3½"

7" 7"

6"

8¼"

9"

2"

25¼"

2¼" 2½" 2¼" 2¼" 2½" 2¼"

Figure A

Inner Mane

1. With right sides together, seam 9″ ends of medium rust rectangle; press seam open. Fold length of fabric in half with wrong sides together. Machine-baste ⅛″ from raw edges; baste again, ¼″ from edges. (Figure B.) Starting at the seam, divide basted edge into quarters and mark with water-soluble pen. Pull gathering threads on mane to fit head.

2. With gathered edge toward neck, pin mane seam to center front face seam at X. (Figure C.) With gathered edge toward back of head, align top of mane (where marked) with center back seam at top of head; pin. Align sides of mane (where marked) with head seam and pin ½″ below ears.

3. Adjusting gathering threads to fit, pin rest of mane to head, aligning ¼″ basting line on mane with head seam and placement line on face. Hand-sew mane to head, using two strands of quilting thread and running stitch.

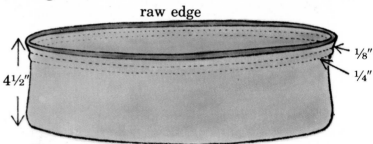

raw edge

4½"

⅛″

¼″

Figure B

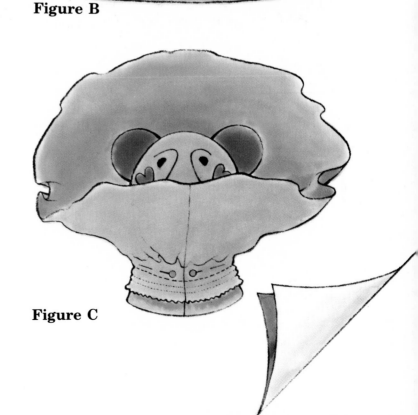

Figure C

Tail

1. With right sides together, sew one 6″ end of light rust rectangle to one 6″ end of dark rust rectangle; press seam open. Fold the rectangle in half lengthwise, right sides together, and seam long edges. Turn tail right side out. Fold entire dark rust rectangle to the inside.

2. Tie the ribbon 3″ from end of tail. Lightly stuff tail and baste opening closed.

Body, Outer Mane, and Lining

1. On body A, machine-baste along six toe lines to within 2″ of bottom edge, as marked. Starting at top of toe lines, machine-baste along center front line all the way to bottom edge. Gather toe lines to 3″ and center front line to 4″; tie off. On wrong side of fabric, sew seam binding behind each line, using regular-length stitches and backstitching at end.

2. With right sides together, sew one outer mane (dark rust rectangle) to top edge of body A; sew other outer mane to top edge of body B. Press seams open. With body A right side up, position basted end of tail ¼″ from bottom edge on right-hand side. (Length of tail should run parallel to bottom edge of fabric.) Pin side edges of body B to body A, right sides together, forming a tube (tail should be inside). Seam side edges; press seams toward body A.

Turn down mane so wrong side faces wrong side of body; press. Machine-baste around mane and body, ⅝″ from raw edge of mane; baste again, ⅜″ from raw edge. Do not gather yet.

3. To form legs, fold tube in half, with right sides still together, on center front line. (Be sure to keep mane out of the

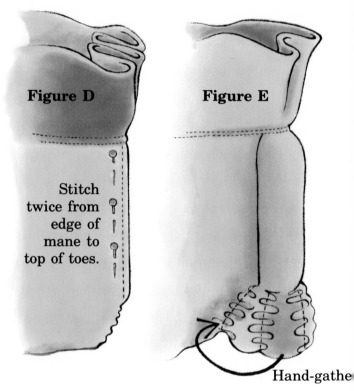

Figure D

Stitch twice from edge of mane to top of toes.

Figure E

Hand-gathe[r]

way.) Fold leg lines to center front line, with pleats toward inside of tube; pin. Sew along edge of fold through all six layers, stitching from edge of mane to top of gathered toes; stitch again to reinforce. (Figure D.)

Seam bottom edge of body, including toes, being careful to keep tail out of the way. Turn body right side out and press.

4. Stuff toes lightly; stuff legs extra-firmly. Using two strands of thread, hand-gather around base of legs to form a puff for feet. To separate feet, start at end of center front line and hand-gather along bottom seam for 3″. (Figure E.) At this point, push needle through foot up to center top of middle toe, back to starting point, up to center top of other middle toe, and back to starting point; tie off.

5. With dark outer mane still on inside of tube, place lion head inside tube. Align leg attachment line on face with ⅝″ gathering line on outer mane. Hand-sew legs

Figure F

to face along line, using two strands of quilting thread and running stitch. (Figure F.) Tack back of head to back of legs.

6. Place lion face down on table and push bottom corner at center back line toward feet. (This will be the lining.)

7. Bring side seams together to form center back; press. Slip-stitch tail to remaining side seam. Open zipper and pin to either side of center back seam, with bottom of zipper just above tail; sew.

8. Use water-soluble pen to mark center back and "side" seams of outer mane.

Gather mane to fit head. Pin center back of mane to top of head; pin side seams to inner mane where inner mane meets head seam. Hand-stitch outer mane to head, using two strands of quilting thread and running stitch.

9. Tack fabric together above top of zipper. To make whiskers, thread needle with two strands of doubled thread. Take small stitch on dot and tie a knot with threads; cut threads to 3½". Repeat for other five dots.

Bow Tie

1. Fold fabric for bow tie with right sides and long edges together; fold with short ends together. Using the ruler and the water-soluble marker, transfer the cutting lines as drawn. Cut out the tie. (Figure G.) Open second fold.

2. With long edges and right sides still together, stitch raw edge, leaving a 2" opening for turning. (Figure H.) Clip the corners. Turn tie right side out and press; slip-stitch opening closed. Place tie around lion's neck, under outer mane, and tie bow in back.

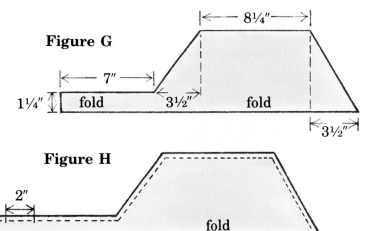

Figure G

Figure H

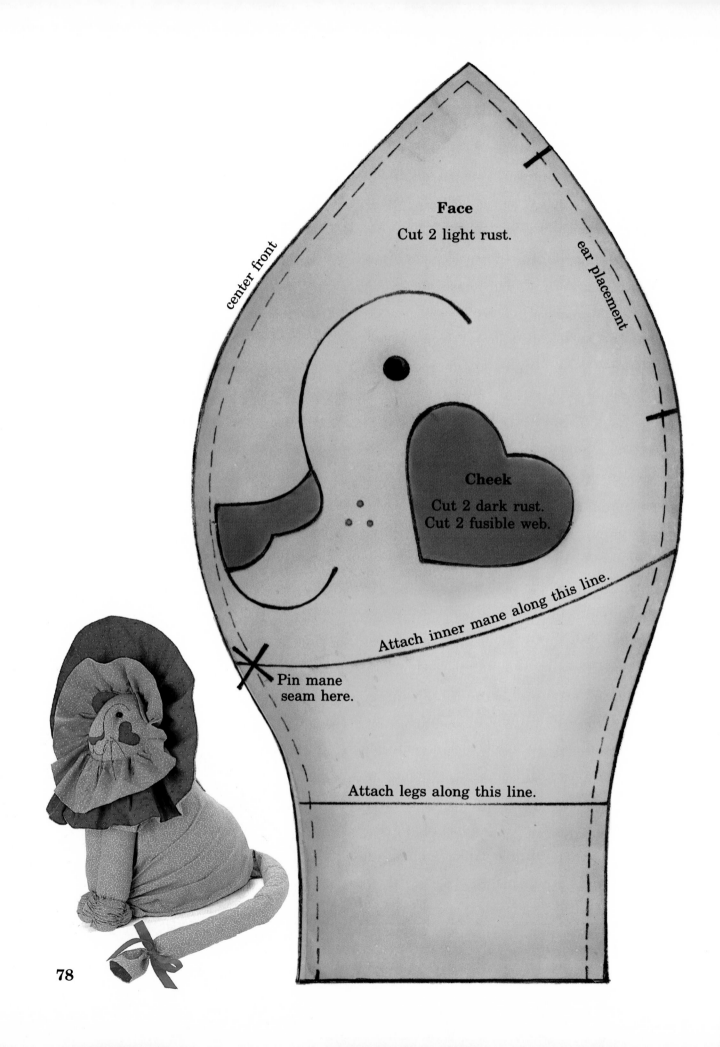

Face
Cut 2 light rust.

center front

ear placement

Cheek

Cut 2 dark rust.
Cut 2 fusible web.

Attach inner mane along this line.

Pin mane
seam here.

Attach legs along this line.

78

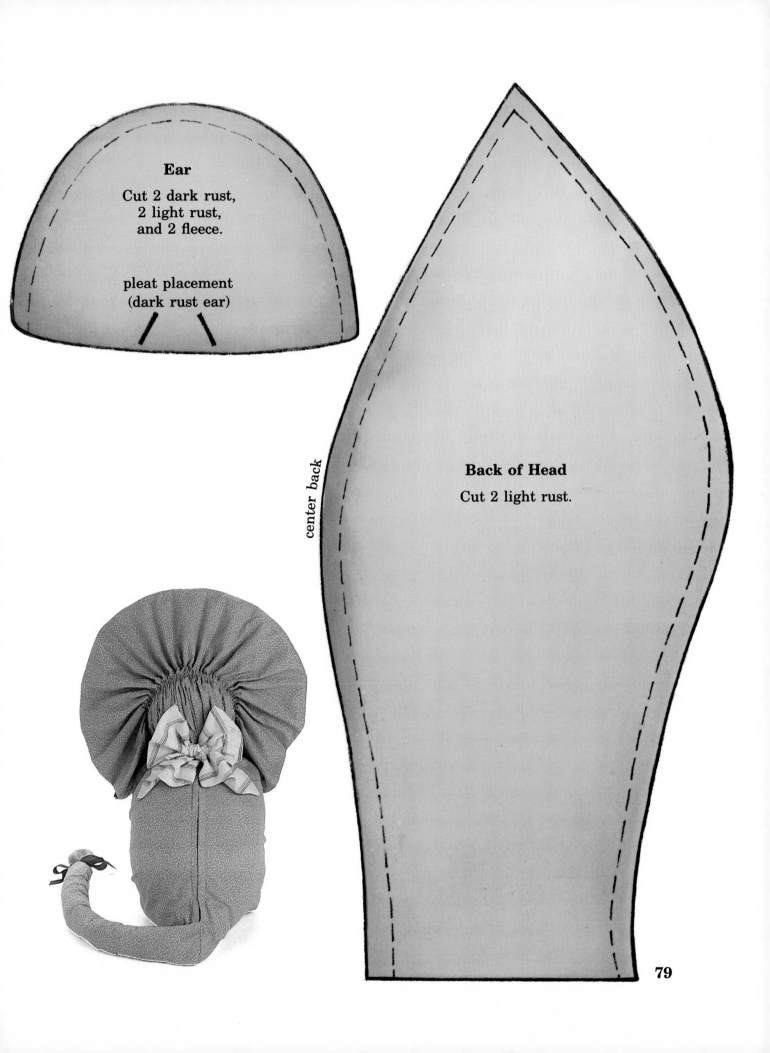

Ear

Cut 2 dark rust,
2 light rust,
and 2 fleece.

pleat placement
(dark rust ear)

center back

Back of Head

Cut 2 light rust.

79

Lighthearted Long Johns

Long underwear for outerwear? It's a natural when sporting counted cross-stitch, especially when the design is as winning as this. What a skating party! Carrot-nosed and brightly bundled up, these frosty fellows cut a fine figure on ice.

Cross-stitch directly on the shirt, using the indentations in the knit as the corners of your stitch. For optimum coverage, use four strands of doubled floss, and to ensure smooth stitches, dampen and separate the strands before threading the needle. When you're through cross-stitching, protect the stitches by backing the design with a piece of lightweight interfacing.

You will need:
white thermal shirt
(prewash and dry to shrink)
water-soluble marking pen
embroidery floss (in colors indicated by color key)
large-eyed needle

1. Find the center front of the shirt neck-line by folding the shirt in half. Mark the center front with the water-soluble pen. Count three rows down from the neck and mark the square directly below the center front mark. This square will be your starting point.

2. Using the colors suggested in the color key, work the design in cross-stitch, be-ginning with the middle snowman. To find the starting point for each outer snowman, count 23 squares from the starting point of the middle one. When you've finished cross-stitching, outline each part of the design, using backstitch and two strands of black floss.

Backstitch the skates, using four strands of doubled floss. Cross-stitch the skating line, starting below the sleeve seam and stitching every other square. To finish, make a French knot for each snow-man's eye with two strands of floss.

3. Gently launder the shirt in mild soap and cold water. Let dry.

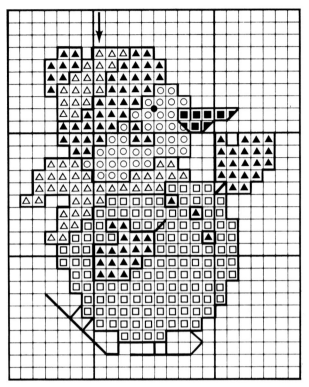

Color Key (DMC)

▲	321	red	□	797	blue
■	741	orange	○		white
△	701	green		310	black

On Your Toes

For a budding ballerina, these togs and tote are a perfect pair. Simple shapes (just two!) and a stick of fabric glue make quick work of the ballet appliqué. Choose a mini-print with a background the same color as the warm-up for the outside of the shoes. Use a stronger shade for the inside of the shoes and a contrasting color for the tote.

Ballet Togs

You will need:
tracing paper
6″ square of solid fabric
8″ square of print fabric
thread to match
warm-up suit
fabric glue stick
2⅔ yards (¼″-wide) ribbon
tear-away backing for appliqué
½ yard (⅛″-wide) ribbon
Fray Check

1. Trace and cut out the patterns for the ballet shoe. Fold the solid fabric in half, right sides together, and cut two inner shoes. Fold the print fabric in half, right sides together, and cut two outer shoes.

2. Arrange the shoe pieces on the shirt front. Cut four 16″ pieces of ¼″-wide ribbon. Glue the shoes in place, tucking two ribbon ends under the heel of each shoe. Pin the loose ribbon ends out of the way.

3. Cut a piece of tear-away backing that is large enough to back both shoes and pin it to the inside of the shirt. Using satin stitch, machine-appliqué the shoes. Carefully tear away the backing.

4. Unpin the ribbon ends. Pull the ribbons loosely to the shoulder of the shirt and bar-tack them in pairs. Cut two 8″ pieces of ⅛″-wide ribbon. Bar-tack each ribbon to the toe of a shoe. Cut two 12″ pieces of ¼″-wide ribbon. Bar-tack each ribbon to a pants cuff.

5. Apply Fray Check to all exposed ribbon ends. Let dry. Tie the ribbons into bows.

Ballet Tote

You will need:
tracing paper
6″ square of solid fabric for appliqué
½ yard (45″-wide) print fabric for appliqué and lining
⅞ yard (45″-wide) solid fabric for bag
thread to match
½ yard of heavyweight interfacing
2⅓ yards (¼″-wide) ribbon
⅓ yard (⅛″-wide) ribbon
4″ x 9¾″ piece of heavy cardboard
Fray Check

1. Trace and cut out the patterns for the ballet shoe. Fold the square of solid fabric in half, right sides together, and cut two inner shoes. Cut one outer shoe from the print fabric; reverse the pattern and cut one more.

Cut a 15¼″ x 29½″ piece from the solid fabric, interfacing, and print fabric. Cut two 3¾″ x 22″ pieces, for handles, from the solid fabric.

Place the piece of fabric for the bag on top of the interfacing and align the edges. Treat these as one piece of fabric. Treat one short end of fabric as top edge.

2. Glue the higher ballet shoe to the fabric so that the heel is 4″ from the top edge and 4″ from the left side. Glue the other ballet shoe 1½″ below the first. Cut the ¼″-wide ribbon in half and position one end of each ribbon under the heel of a shoe.

Using satin stitch, machine-sew along the edges of the shoes. Cut the ⅛″-wide ribbon in half. Bar-tack a ribbon to the toe of each shoe.

3. Fold the fabric for the bag in half, top to bottom, with right sides together. Seam the side edges of the fabric, using a ⅝″ seam allowance. Do not turn.

Stand the bag up to form a flat bottom, creating a triangle of excess fabric on each side. Sew a seam across each triangle where the base measures 4″. (Figure A.) Cut off the triangles ⅝″ below the seams. Do not turn.

4. Fold each handle in half lengthwise with right sides together and sew, using a ⅝″ seam allowance. Turn the handles right side out. Center the seam on the back of each handle; press. Topstitch along the handles ⅛″ from each long edge.

With the bag still turned inside out, pin the ends of one handle to the front of the bag, right sides together, so that the ends of the handle are even with the top of the bag and 4″ from the side seams. (Figure B.) Sew the ends to the bag, using a ⅝″ seam allowance and being careful not to twist the handle. Sew the other handle in the same way to the back of the bag.

Turn the bag right side out. Turn down the top edge of the bag 1½″. (The handles will turn up.) Put the piece of cardboard in the bottom of the bag.

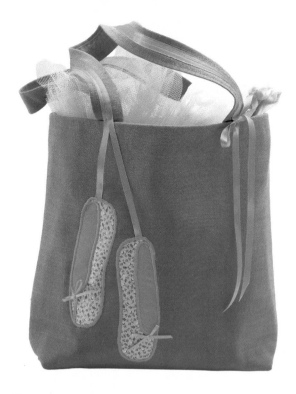

5. Repeat Step 3 to make the lining.

6. Turn back top edge of lining 1½″. Put the lining inside the bag. Pin the lining to the bag so that the fold of the lining is about ⅛″ below the top of the bag. Sew the lining to the bag ¼″ from the top; stitch again, ½″ from the top.

7. Pull the ribbons that are attached to the shoes loosely up to the handle. Pin the ribbons the length of the handle, overlapping them and making sure that they lie flat. Sew the ribbons down the center and outer edges. Secure the ribbons by sewing across them where the handle ends meet the bag.

8. Apply Fray Check to all exposed ribbon ends. Let dry. Tie the ribbons into bows.

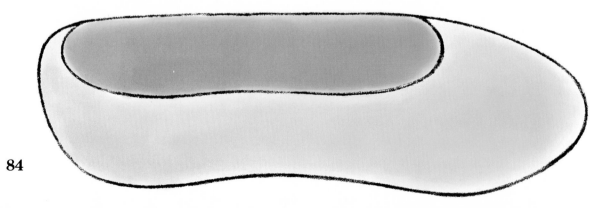

Shooting Stars

It used to be cowboy suits, trucks, and trains, but these days robots top the list of what little boys want most. Add this appliquéd version to a kid's collection. It's bound to be a favorite—and so will you!

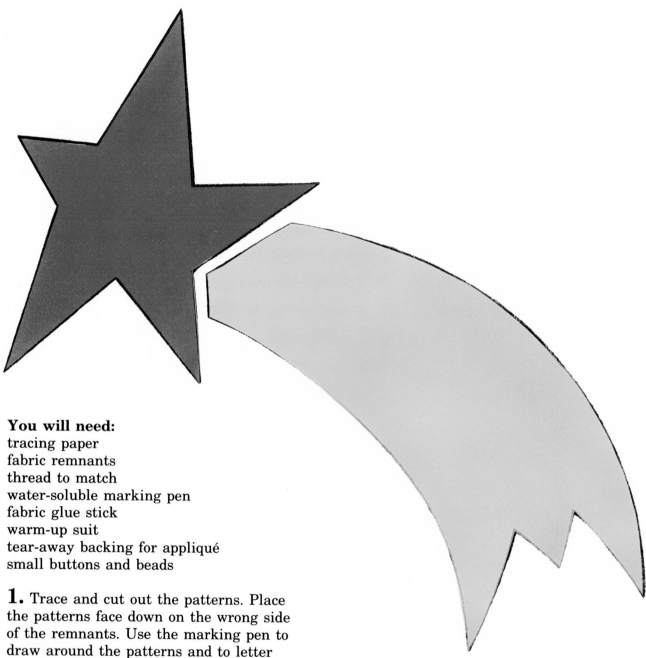

You will need:
tracing paper
fabric remnants
thread to match
water-soluble marking pen
fabric glue stick
warm-up suit
tear-away backing for appliqué
small buttons and beads

1. Trace and cut out the patterns. Place the patterns face down on the wrong side of the remnants. Use the marking pen to draw around the patterns and to letter the pieces. Cut out the pieces.

2. Glue the pieces to the shirt and pants. Cut three pieces of tear-away backing large enough to back the robot and the two shooting stars. Pin the pieces of backing to the inside of the shirt and pants.

3. Machine-appliqué the robot and stars, using satin stitch. Press the appliquéd pieces, using a damp cloth and warm iron. Gently tear away the backing.

4. Sew buttons and beads onto the robot for eyes and control knobs, as marked on the pattern. Use contrasting thread to hand-stitch the readout on the robot's lower control panel.

Note: To launder the appliquéd suit, machine-wash in cold water on the gentle cycle. Line dry.

T-Shirt Sleepshirts

Turn T-shirts into sleepshirts with one-of-a-kind art and eyelet trim. No mixing, no mess—applying paint to fabric is easy with ballpoint tubes. Place a piece of fine-grit sandpaper inside the shirt, behind the design, before you begin painting. The sandpaper will keep the ballpoint rolling, add a textured look to the painted fabric, and absorb the excess paint.

You will need:
embroidery transfer pencil
piece of tracing or typing paper
iron
man's all-cotton T-shirt
fine-grit sandpaper
ballpoint paint tubes in assorted colors
gingham-edged eyelet trim
9″ (¼″-wide) ribbon

1. Using the embroidery transfer pencil, draw a stick figure on the piece of paper.

2. Preheat the iron for five minutes on a medium-hot setting. Center the drawing, face down, on the front of the T-shirt. Slowly iron the drawing to transfer it.

3. Place the piece of sandpaper inside the shirt, behind the drawing. Color the drawing with the ballpoint paint, following the directions on the tube. Personalize the shirt, if desired.

4. Cut a piece of eyelet that is a little longer than the length needed to trim the edge of the shirt bottom. Pin and then sew the edge of the eyelet to the edge of the shirt, turning under and overlapping the ends of the eyelet. Cut a piece of eyelet for each shirt sleeve and sew these in the same way. Tack the ribbon to the stick figure's hair and tie a bow.

Traffic Stopper

Looking terrific, this tyke is all set to take his teddy for a spin. What a sporty car—and what a spiffy sweater!

Duplicate-stitch embroidery is a quick way to add interest to a sweater, and mastering the technique will take only minutes. Use yarn of a similar weight to that which was used to knit the sweater. Pull your stitches carefully so that the embroidery completely covers the knitted stitches without altering the tension.

You will need:
sweater (ready-made or hand-knitted)
tapestry needle
yarn in yellow, green, red, and black
white embroidery floss
6 (¾″) buttons

1. To stitch the middle car, match center of design to center front of sweater.

2. Starting from the wrong side of the sweater and leaving about a 4″ tail of yarn, pull the needle up through the stitch that is below the one to be covered. (Figure A.) Pass the needle from right to left under the stitch that is above the one to be covered. (Figure A.) Reinsert the needle into the stitch through which you originally pulled the needle. (Figure B.)

3. Follow the graph to complete the car. When finished, weave the ends of the yarn through several stitches on the back of the sweater.

4. Stitch the side cars (one green and one red), referring to photograph for placement. Stitch the sign on one sleeve and the traffic light on the other. Using outline stitch and six strands of embroidery floss, write STOP on the sign. Sew buttons on the cars for wheels.

Color Key

○	yellow
△	green
■	red
●	black

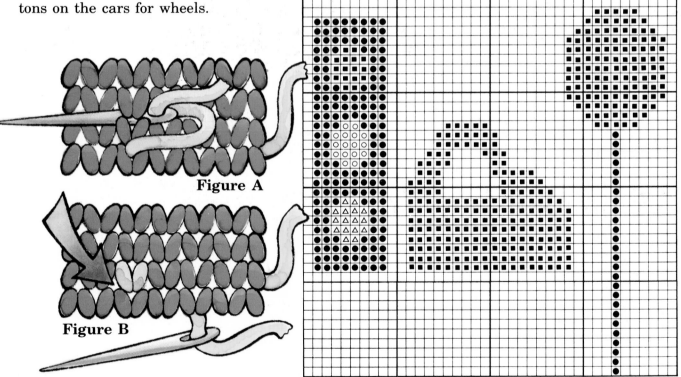

Figure A

Figure B

An Overall Great Idea

No doubt about it, Christmas fashions are fun—but the wearing season is short. Somehow it seems a shame to pack away clothing that's only been worn a couple of weeks. One super solution? This tree-trimmed bib for overalls. Button it on before Santa comes, and once he's gone, just take it off!

You will need:
pair of overalls
tracing paper
½ yard (45″-wide) white fabric for bib
½ yard (45″-wide) white lining
scraps of print fabric for appliqué
thread to match
fabric glue stick
tear-away backing for appliqué
water-soluble marking pen
package of piping

1. To make a pattern for the Christmas bib, fold the bib of the overalls in half lengthwise. Align one long edge of the tracing paper with the bib fold. Draw a line around the bib, ½″ outside the edge. Mark horizontal placement for the button-holes and remove the tracing paper. Draw a line outside the first line, ⅝″ from it. Cut out the pattern.

Fold the bib fabric and the lining in half. Cut one bib from each, aligning the fabric fold with the long straight edge of the pattern.

2. Transfer the patterns for the tree, tree skirt, and presents to the scraps of print fabric. Cut out the pieces and glue them to the front of the bib, centering the tree. Cut a piece of backing large enough to back the appliqué. Pin the backing to the back of the bib.

3. Using satin stitch, machine-sew the appliqué. Use the marking pen to draw the star, garland, tree trunk, and ribbons. Satin-stitch these. Carefully tear away the backing.

4. Cut a piece of piping that is long enough to go around the bib. Baste the piping to the front of the bib so that the ends of the piping meet at the bottom of the bib. Using a zipper foot and leaving a 3″ opening for turning at the bottom, stitch the right side of the lining to the right side of the bib, with the piping in between. Clip the corners and trim all seams, except the 3″ opening, to ¼″. Turn the bib right side out and press the piping. Topstitch ⅛″ from the piped edge. Make the buttonholes.

5. Rinse the bib in plain water to remove the markings. Gently launder the bib in mild soap and cold water. Let dry; press.

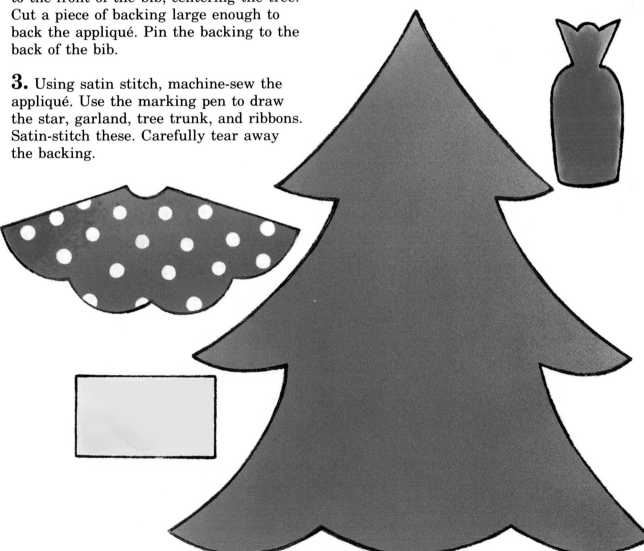

What-to-Do Shoe

Home, sweet home is a big blue shoe for this well-known lady and her energetic crew.

You will need:

brown paper for pattern
tape measure
tracing paper
½ yard solid blue fabric
⅓ yard blue plaid fabric
2″ x 13″ piece of brown fabric
½ yard solid white fabric
2½″ x 14″ piece of red polka dot fabric
scrap of solid red fabric
scrap of blue print fabric
thread to match
water-soluble marking pen
polyester stuffing
6 (1″) plastic rings
42″ (¾″-wide) red shoestring
peach acrylic paint
artist's brush
razor-point permanent markers (black and
    red)
perle cotton (black, orange, yellow, brown,
    and gray)
½ yard (⅛″-wide) red polka-dot ribbon

1. Enlarge patterns for the sock and shoe (includes sole) to full size on brown paper, adding ¼″ seam allowances. Cut out the patterns; pin to fabrics and cut as marked. Using the water-soluble pen, transfer pattern markings to shoe. From remaining solid blue fabric, cut three 3½″ squares for pockets.

Trace patterns for the doll, doll clothes, and heart, adding ¼″ seam allowances. Pin patterns to fabrics and cut as marked.

2. On each blue square, press the top edge under ¼″ and sew, stitching close to the edge; press the side and bottom edges under ¼″. Pin the squares to the shoe front. Sew the side and bottom edges of the squares to the shoe, stitching the edges close to the fold.

3. Turn under the top edge of the shoe sole ¼″. With bottom edges of shoe and shoe sole aligned, pin the folded edge of the shoe sole to the shoe front. Zigzag-stitch the folded edge.

With right sides together, pin shoe front to shoe back and sew as marked. Turn under edges of opening ¼″, then ¼″ again; press and sew. Turn shoe and press. Firmly stuff bottom of shoe to 1″ below the opening with polyester stuffing.

4. Pin the sock pieces with right sides together. Sew the top and sides, leaving the bottom open. Turn and stuff the sock. Turn under the bottom edges ¼″ and machine-stitch closed. Slip the sock into the shoe. Add extra stuffing to the shoe, if needed. Tack the sock to the shoe at the beginning and end of the shoe seam.

5. Tack the plastic rings to either side of the shoe as marked, sewing around each ring at the top, sides, and bottom. Lace and tie shoestring.

6. Pin the hearts with right sides together and sew, leaving opening as marked. Clip curves; turn heart and press. Turn under raw edge of opening and sew closed. Appliqué the heart to the shoe.

7. Pin the clothes to the doll fronts. On each doll, zigzag-stitch the edges of the neck and sleeves. On the girls, zigzag the bottom of the dresses; on the boys, zigzag the waist and legs of the shorts.

With right sides together, pin doll fronts to doll backs and sew, leaving bottom edge open. Clip the curves and corners. Turn dolls; press and stuff. Turn under bottom edge of dolls and sew opening closed.

8. Lightly pencil the hairline on each

doll's face, using the photograph as a guide. Paint the faces, arms, and hands with peach paint and let dry. Using the black marker, draw eyes and a mouth on each doll; draw glasses on the Old Lady. Draw and color the heart cheeks with the red marker.

Using perle cotton, satin-stitch the hair. For the Old Lady's bun, sew a series of French knots. For the girls' pigtails, sew loops; cut the loops if desired. Cut pieces of ribbon and tie them into bows. Sew the bows to the pigtails.

Add ¼″ seam allowances to all patterns.

Doll

Cut 16 white.

Leave open.

Dress

For girls, cut 4 short from red polka dot.

For old lady, cut 1 long from blue print.

Shirt

Cut 3 red.

Shorts

Cut 3 red polka dot.

Heart

Cut 2 red.

Leave open.

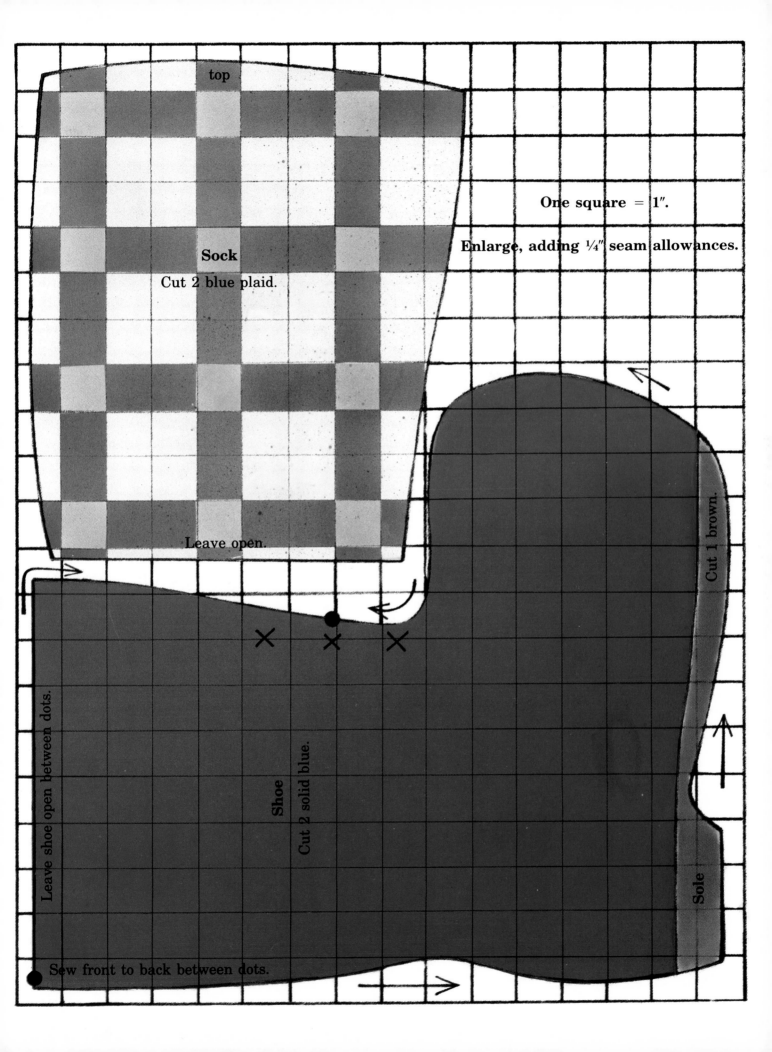

top

Sock

Cut 2 blue plaid.

One square = 1″.

Enlarge, adding ¼″ seam allowances.

Cut 1 brown.

Leave open.

Shoe

Cut 2 solid blue.

Leave shoe open between dots.

Sole

Sew front to back between dots.

Little Miss Molly

Meet Molly, an endearing doll who'll take delight in playing school, having tea, and being tucked in bed.

You will need:
tracing paper
½ yard (36″-wide) muslin for doll
1 yard (36″-wide) print fabric for dress
small piece of satin for shoes
2 yards (1″-wide) eyelet trim
1 yard (½″-wide) flat lace trim
⅓ yard (⅜″-wide) heart lace trim
thread to match
water-soluble marking pen
tape measure
embroidery floss (pink, brown, blue, white, and black)

soft red pencil
polyester stuffing
mohair yarn for hair
large-eyed needle
hook and eye
¼ yard (¼″-wide) elastic
2 heart buttons
½ yard (⅞″-wide) satin ribbon

Note: Use ¼″ seam allowance throughout unless instructed otherwise.

Making the Doll

1. Trace and cut out patterns for the doll, adding ¼″ seam allowances. Pin patterns to muslin and cut as marked. Using the water-soluble pen, transfer pattern markings, including facial features.

2. Embroider facial features, using colors and embroidery stitches indicated. Lightly color cheeks with red pencil.

3. Pin head with right sides together and sew, leaving neck open. Clip curves; turn head right side out and press. Stuff head firmly with polyester stuffing.

4. Pin body with right sides together and sew, leaving openings as marked. Clip curves; turn body. Press and stuff.

5. Pin arms and then legs with right sides together; sew, leaving openings as marked. Clip curves; turn limbs. Press and stuff.

6. To attach head to body, turn edge of neck opening on body to inside ¼″. Insert raw edge of neck; pin and hand-sew as marked.

To attach the arms, turn edge of arm openings on body to inside ¼″. Insert raw edge of arms, aligning arm seams with body seams; pin and hand-sew as marked.

To attach legs, turn bottom edge of body to inside ¼″. Insert raw edge of legs, aligning legs with sides of body; pin and hand-sew as marked. Sew opening closed.

7. To make hair, use a double strand of yarn and the large-eyed needle. (Do not knot yarn.) Working from left to right, make a horizontal row of loops as shown. At end of row, turn doll and begin next row, working again from left to right. For bangs, trim loops close to head.

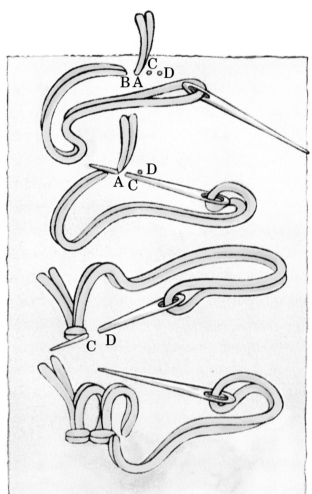

Making the Hair

1. Insert needle at A and pull out at B. Pull thread through, leaving a 1″ tail above the stitch.

2. With thread below the needle, insert needle at C and pull out at A, pulling thread tightly to make a small locking stitch.

3. With thread above the needle, insert needle at D and pull out at C, leaving a ½″ loop above the stitch.

4. Continue stitching row, alternating locking stitches and loops.

Making the Dress and Shoes

1. From print fabric, cut two 4½" x 16" rectangles for bodice and sleeves. Fold one bodice piece with short edges together and mark center of one long edge on wrong side of fabric. For neck opening, mark 2" on either side of the center mark. This bodice piece will be the back.

2. Pin top long edge of back bodice to one long edge of front bodice with right sides together. For top sleeve seams, sew from one end of long edge to 2" mark; sew from other end to 2" mark. Press open all the way across.

Starting at center mark, draw a 3" line down bodice back. Cut along the line to make bodice opening. Turn under raw edges of neck and bodice openings ¼" and press.

Cut an 8½" piece of eyelet and sew to inside edge of neck, turning under ends of eyelet; sew edges of bodice opening. Sew hook and eye to neck at bodice opening.

3. Turn under wrist edge of sleeves ½" and press; sew, stitching close to raw edge to make casing. Cut two 8½" pieces of eyelet and sew to inside edge of wrists. Measure doll's wrist and cut two pieces of elastic, each ½" shorter than measurement. Run elastic through casings and tack ends of elastic to sleeves.

4. With right sides of front and back bodice together, sew one bottom sleeve seam, stitching from edge of wrist for 3¼"; sew remaining sleeve seam in same way. Press seams open.

5. For the skirt, cut two 10½" x 16" rectangles and sew together at short edges. Press seams open. Baste along one long edge of skirt and gather to fit bodice. With right sides together, pin skirt to bodice, aligning side seams of skirt with underarm seams; adjust gathers and sew, using ⅜" seam allowance. Press seam toward bodice. Clip where necessary. Turn dress right side out and press.

6. Turn up hem of dress 1" and press; turn under raw edge ¼" and sew. Cut a 32" piece of flat lace and sew along stitching; trim end of lace. Cut a 32" piece of eyelet and sew along inside edge of hem, turning under the ends of the eyelet.

7. Cut a 12" piece of eyelet and a 12" piece of heart lace. Pin the eyelet in U-shape to the bodice front, turning under the ends; baste. Pin the lace over the eyelet, trimming the excess lace. Sew, stitching through the three layers. Turn down eyelet at shoulder seams and at center front and tack to bodice. Sew on the heart buttons. Place dress on doll and tie ribbon around waist.

8. Trace the shoe pattern. Pin pattern to satin and cut as marked. Pin shoe pieces in pairs with right sides together and sew. Trim seams and clip curves; turn. Fold top edge of shoe to inside ⅜" and sew by hand; press. Place shoes on feet.

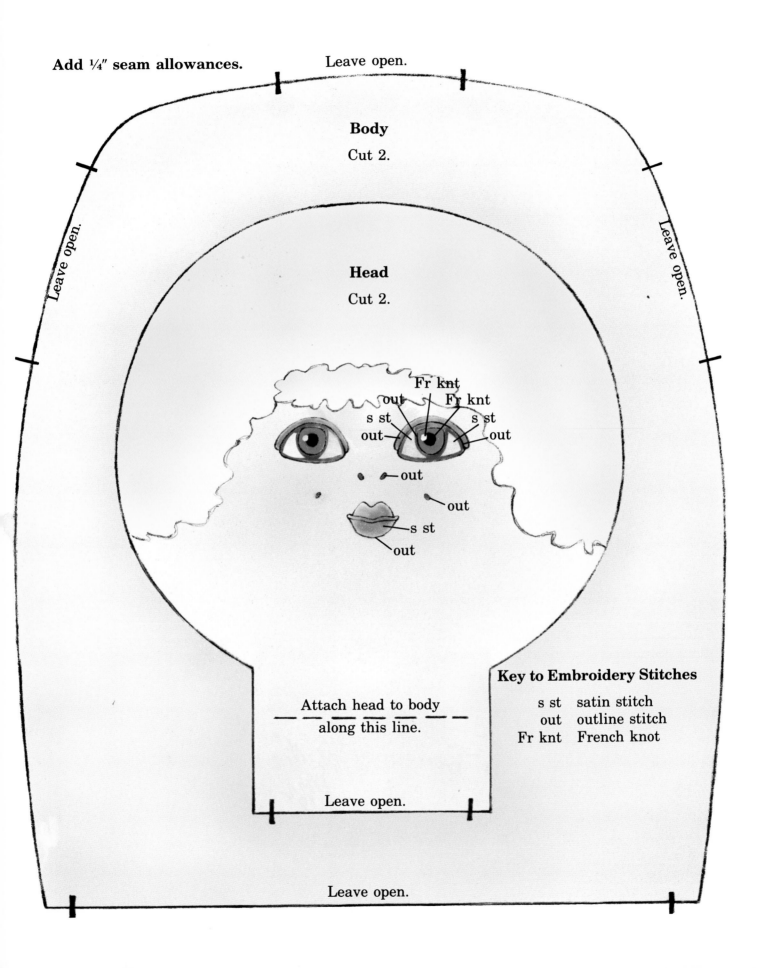

Add ¼″ seam allowances.

Leave open.

Body
Cut 2.

Leave open.

Leave open.

Head
Cut 2.

Fr knt
out
Fr knt
s st
s st
out
out
out
out
s st
out

Attach head to body
along this line.

Key to Embroidery Stitches

s st   satin stitch
out   outline stitch
Fr knt   French knot

Leave open.

Leave open.

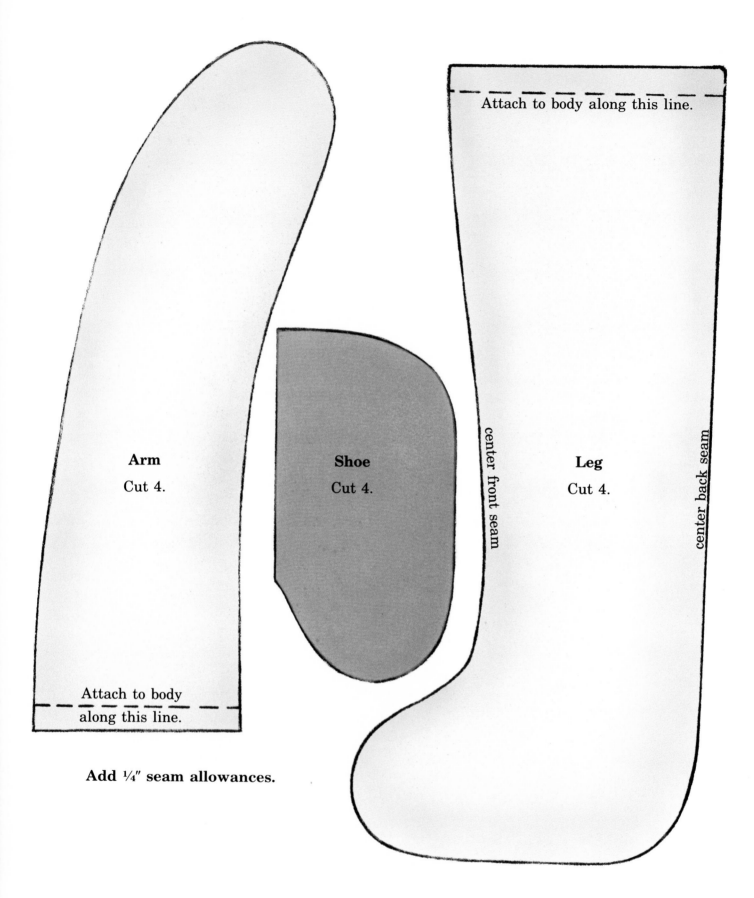

Arm

Cut 4.

Attach to body
along this line.

Add ¼″ seam allowances.

Shoe

Cut 4.

center front seam

Leg

Cut 4.

Attach to body along this line.

center back seam

102

Corner Cabin

Standing in the corner can be fun, when the corner is covered with a cabin like this. Made of felt, the playhouse stands six feet tall at the peak and measures 34″ across each of the two sides. Artist's stretcher strips, joined and glued together, form the almost ready-made frame that is used to support the wall-hung house.

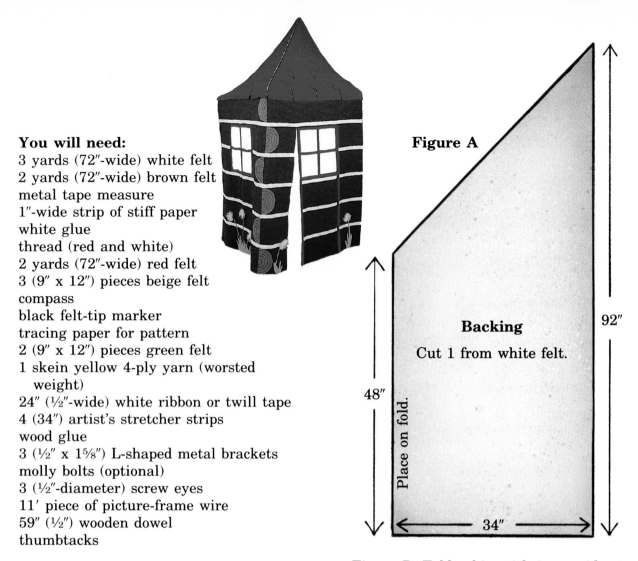

You will need:
3 yards (72″-wide) white felt
2 yards (72″-wide) brown felt
metal tape measure
1″-wide strip of stiff paper
white glue
thread (red and white)
2 yards (72″-wide) red felt
3 (9″ x 12″) pieces beige felt
compass
black felt-tip marker
tracing paper for pattern
2 (9″ x 12″) pieces green felt
1 skein yellow 4-ply yarn (worsted
  weight)
24″ (½″-wide) white ribbon or twill tape
4 (34″) artist's stretcher strips
wood glue
3 (½″ x 1⅝″) L-shaped metal brackets
molly bolts (optional)
3 (½″-diameter) screw eyes
11′ piece of picture-frame wire
59″ (½″) wooden dowel
thumbtacks

Figure A

Backing
Cut 1 from white felt.

92″

48″

Place on fold.

← 34″ →

Making the Cabin

1. From white felt, cut backing for cabin and roof. (Figure A.) From brown felt, cut six 7″ x 68″ strips for logs.

Glue first log along bottom edge of white felt backing. Using the strip of stiff paper as a measure, glue second log 1″ above first log. Continue gluing logs 1″ apart, ending 47″ from bottom edge of backing. When glue has dried, fold cabin with inner sides together and press on fold to form outside corner of cabin.

2. From white felt, cut a 2″ x 68″ facing strip. On inside of cabin, pin top edge of facing strip 1″ above top log; edge-stitch top edge (only) of strip to cabin.

3. From red felt, cut five strips for one side of roof, using measurements given in

Figure B. Fold cabin with inner sides together. Position first roof strip over top log so that 5½″ of the log remains visible; glue top edge of strip to backing. Position second roof strip so that bottom edge is 7″ from bottom edge of first strip, and glue top edge to backing. Overlap and glue remaining strips in same way as second strip. Cut away ends of roof strips along edge of backing. (Figure B.) Cut five strips for other side of roof and glue to backing in same way; cut away ends of strips. On both sides of roof, glue edges of strips to backing.

4. On bottom red strip on one side of roof, measure 8½″ from straight edge and mark a cutting line. (Figure B.) On same strip, mark two more lines 8½″ apart. On strip above bottom one, stagger the lines by marking the first line 4¼″ from edge.

104

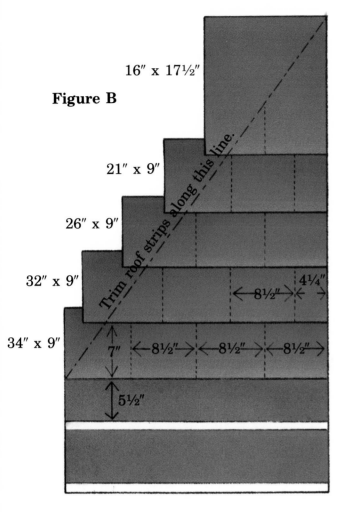

16" x 17½"

Figure B

21" x 9"

26" x 9"

32" x 9"

34" x 9"

Trim roof strips along this line.

4¼"

←8½"→←

7" ←8½"→←8½"→←8½"→

5½"

Continue marking roof strips as shown. (Figure B.) Mark strips in same way on other side of roof.

Cut along lines to make shingles, ending each cut at bottom edge of overlapping strip. Spot-glue shingles, about 3" from bottom edge, to backing.

5. From beige felt, cut three 8" circles. Cut circles in half to make log ends. Using the black marker, draw growth lines on the log ends, following curve of log. Glue log ends to six of the logs, referring to photograph for placement.

6. From red felt, cut two 15" squares for windows and two 1" x 24" strips for the door. From each window, cut out four 6" squares to make panes. (Figure C.) Center, then glue, a window over the fourth and fifth logs on each side of the cabin.

On right side of cabin, glue door strips beneath window. (See photograph.) When glue is dry, cut away layers of brown and white felt behind window panes. To form door opening, cut through both layers of felt along left edge of door and window, cutting from bottom of door to within ½" of top of window.

7. Transfer pattern for grass and flower stems to green felt. Cut one complete unit and two single flower stems as marked. Glue complete grass unit to bottom left side of cabin. Glue single stems on each side of cabin door.

From yellow yarn, cut ten pieces, each three yards long. Working with two pieces at once, wrap yarn in a figure eight around thumb and little finger. Cut a 5" piece of yarn and tie it tightly around center of wrapped yarn; cut loop ends. Arrange ends in a circle and trim to form flower about 3" in diameter. Repeat to make four more flowers. Glue flowers to top of stems.

8. From white felt, cut a 3" x 60" strip. To form casing, fold strip with long edges together and sew ⅜" from long edge. Trim seam to ¼".

Fold ribbon in half and position ribbon fold on stitched edge of casing 2" from

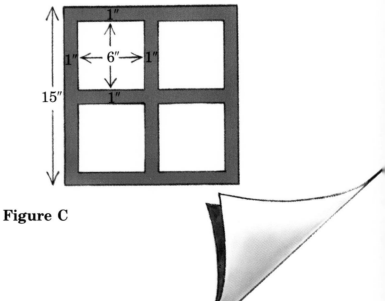

1"

1" ←6"→ 1"

15"

1"

Figure C

top. On inside of roof, sandwich ribbon fold and stitched edge of casing between slanted edges of roof (casing and ends of ribbon should be on inside of roof); pin. Trim away pointed top of roof (about ½″), just above casing. Sew together slanted edges of roof with casing and ribbon fold between, stitching along edge of roof strips from top of roof to corner at top of walls.

Hanging the Cabin

1. Join stretcher strips to form a square; glue corners with wood glue. Attach brackets to top of strips and insert two screw eyes as shown in Figure D. With frame parallel to floor and 45″ from it, attach brackets to wall, using molly bolts if necessary.

2. Insert remaining screw eye in corner of wall, 27″ above frame. Thread one end of wire through one screw eye on frame and wrap securely, as for a picture. Run other end of wire through screw eye in corner of wall; run wire through eye again, checking first to make sure frame is still parallel with floor. Thread wire through remaining screw eye on frame and wrap end securely. (Figure D.)

3. Slide dowel into roof casing and place cabin over frame. Working from inside frame, attach facing strip to top of frame with thumbtacks, clipping facing strip at corner of frame and around screw eyes. (Figure E.) At top of roof, pull one ribbon end through screw eye on wall; tie ribbon ends and secure with knot.

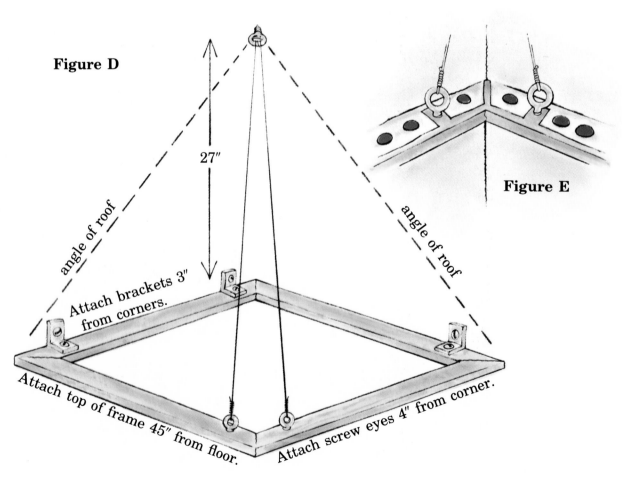

Figure D

27″

angle of roof

angle of roof

Figure E

Attach brackets 3″ from corners.

Attach top of frame 45″ from floor.

Attach screw eyes 4″ from corner.

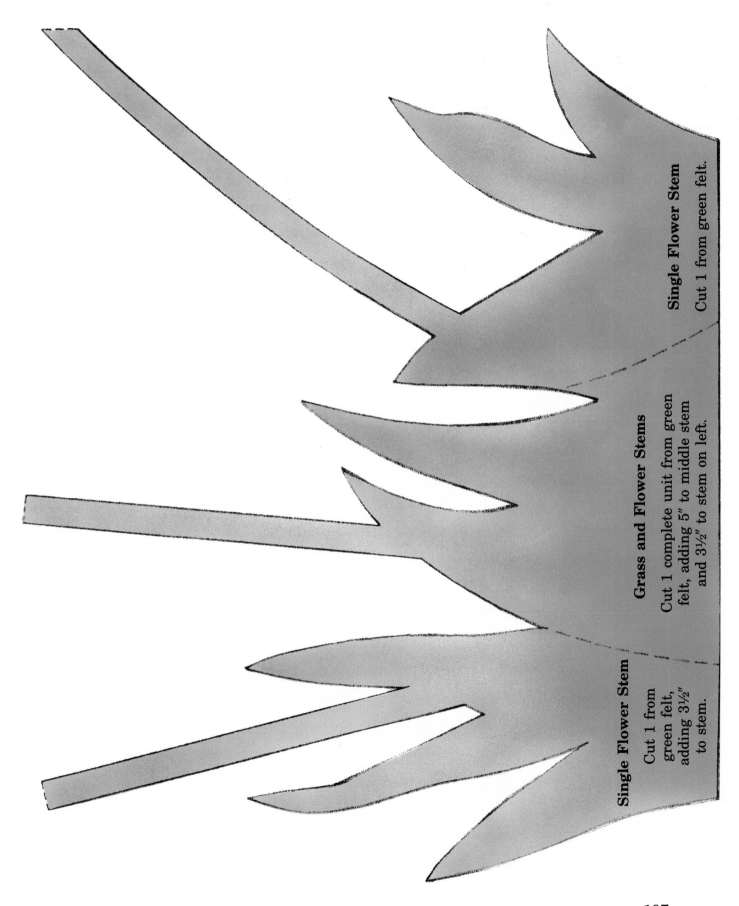

Single Flower Stem

Cut 1 from green felt, adding 3½" to stem.

Grass and Flower Stems

Cut 1 complete unit from green felt, adding 5" to middle stem and 3½" to stem on left.

Single Flower Stem

Cut 1 from green felt.

Paddle Ball Game

Great gifts for giving groups or stuffing in stockings, paddle ball games are quick, easy, and inexpensive to make— and they're sure to be a big hit with kids!

You will need:
tracing paper
7″ x 10½″ (¼″) plywood
electric saber saw
sandpaper
paintbrushes
enamel undercoat
carbon paper
high-gloss enamel paint
  (assorted colors)
stapler
16″ piece of elastic string
small rubber ball

1. Trace the pattern (including features) and cut it out.

2. On the back (rough side) of the plywood, place the pattern face down and draw around it. Using the saber saw, cut out the paddle.

3. Sand the paddle until smooth, sanding with the grain. Paint the paddle with enamel undercoat and let dry; sand lightly again. Paint the paddle white and let dry.

4. Using carbon paper, transfer features to front of paddle. Paint the features, applying several coats of paint and allowing the paint to dry after each application.

5. Staple one end of the string to the ball and the other end to the clown's nose.

109

Pigtail Jumprope

Skipping rope will be twice the fun with these pigtailed cuties in hand. Unbleached muslin gives the friendly faces a fresh-scrubbed look that's set aglow with pink heart cheeks and a happy smile.

You will need:
tracing paper
¼ yard unbleached muslin
small piece of pink felt
2 (3") squares of print fabric
thread to match
water-soluble marking pen
fabric glue stick
red embroidery floss
4 large black beads
polyester stuffing
rope (about 6')
5" (1"-wide) eyelet trim
2 heart buttons
cotton yarn
large-eyed needle
2" x 4" piece of cardboard
1⅓ yard (¼"-wide) ribbon

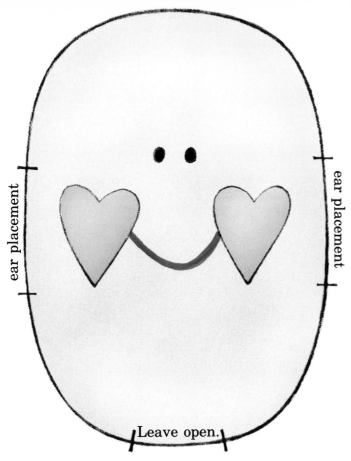

ear placement

ear placement

Leave open.

Add ¼″ seam allowances to patterns
for face and ear.

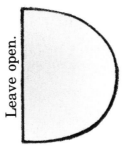

Leave open.

1. Trace and cut out the patterns for the face, ear, and heart cheeks, adding ¼″ seam allowances to face and ear. From muslin, cut four faces and eight ears. Cut four cheeks from felt. Using the water-soluble pen, mark placement of ears, cheeks, facial features, and neck opening on two of the faces.

2. Glue the cheeks to the faces as marked; appliqué the cheeks by hand or machine. Using the red floss and outline stitch, embroider the mouths. Sew on the beads for eyes.

3. Pin ears in pairs with right sides together and sew, leaving straight edge open. Clip curves; turn ears and press.

4. With right sides together and raw edges aligned, pin ears to faces as marked. Pin these faces to plain faces with right sides together and sew, leaving openings as marked. Clip curves; turn faces and press. Stuff faces with polyester stuffing.

5. Turn under the side and bottom edges of the fabric squares ¼″ and press. Wrap and pin the squares around the rope 2″ from the ends, placing the top (raw edge) of the squares toward ends of rope. Sew the squares to the rope, stitching along the side and bottom edges of the squares.

6. On one stuffed face, turn under edge of neck opening ¼″ and insert 2½″ of one rope end. Securely sew the face to the rope, sewing through the rope and closing the opening. Turn under edge of neck opening on other face; sew face to other end of rope in same way.

7. Cut the eyelet in half and sew pieces to bottom edge of faces, turning under ends of the eyelet. Sew a heart button in the center of each piece of eyelet.

8. To make the bangs, use a single strand of yarn and the large-eyed needle. Sew loops (see figure on page 99) to top of head along seam. Cut the loops.

To make each of the four pigtails, wrap a piece of yarn lengthwise 25 times around the 2″ x 4″ piece of cardboard. At one end of the cardboard, tie a piece of yarn around the loops; cut the loops at the other end. Sew the pigtails to the head. Cut four 12″ pieces of ribbon and tie these around the pigtails.

Lullaby Time

A dolly needs to rest as well as play, and here's a dreamy place to lay a dolly's sleepy head. Made of ¾″ plywood, the cradle is sturdy and measures a roomy 25″ from end to end and 17″ across. The comfy, eyelet-edged quilt is pieced in strips and features a scalloped border that's repeated in the matching pillowcase.

Rock-A-Bye Cradle

You will need:
poster paper
yardstick
4′ x 4′ (¾″) best-grade plywood
sandpaper
electric saber saw
16 (1½″ to 2″) #8 wood screws
¼″ electric drill with countersink and ⁹⁄₆₄″
  bits
wood filler
paintbrushes
enamel undercoat
carbon paper
high-gloss enamel paint (white, blue, and
  yellow)
gray fine-tip paint marker (oil base)

Note: Assemble the cradle with smooth side of wood pieces facing out. Countersink the wood screws, using the countersink bit to drill a hole for the screw head and the ⁹⁄₆₄″ bit to drill a hole for the screw shaft.

1. Enlarge pattern for cradle ends to full size on poster paper. Cut out the pattern. Mark the front A and the back B.

2. On the back (rough side) of the plywood, draw around side A of the pattern, then side B. Draw two 10″ x 24″ rectangles for the cradle sides and one 10¼″ x 24″ rectangle for the cradle bottom. Using

the saber saw, carefully cut out the pieces. Sand edges of the cut pieces.

3. Stand one cradle end on flat work surface. With assistance, place one cradle side in position for attachment and mark placement for the screws on the cradle end. (See figure.) Drill holes and insert screws, one at a time. Place second cradle side in position and attach to cradle end in same way. Repeat procedure for attaching other cradle end to cradle sides.

4. Position the cradle bottom between the cradle sides so that it rests on the sides. Mark the location of cradle bottom on the front of the cradle ends. Attach each cradle end to the cradle bottom with two wood screws.

5. Use wood filler to fill all cracks and holes; let dry. Sand the cradle smooth and paint with enamel undercoat; let dry. Sand lightly again. Paint the cradle with two coats of white enamel, letting the paint dry after each application.

6. Draw sun on one end of cradle and moon and stars on other end, using patterns and photographs as a guide. Sketch bottom of cloud on each end. Paint the cradle ends and let dry. Outline design with gray marker.

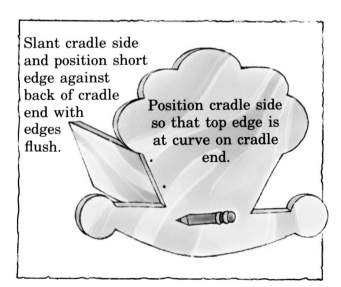

Slant cradle side and position short edge against back of cradle end with edges flush.

Position cradle side so that top edge is at curve on cradle end.

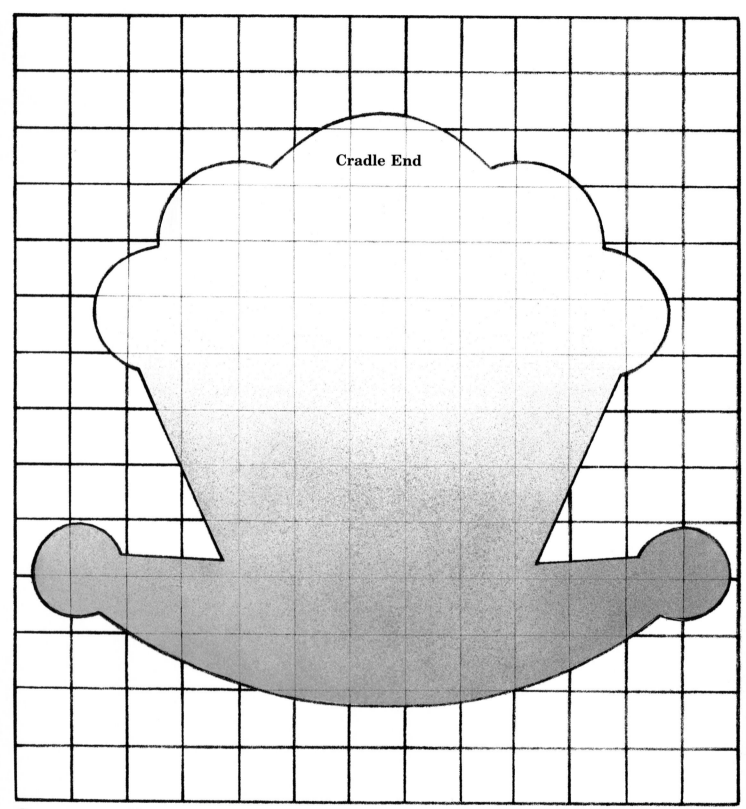

Cradle End

One square = 2″.

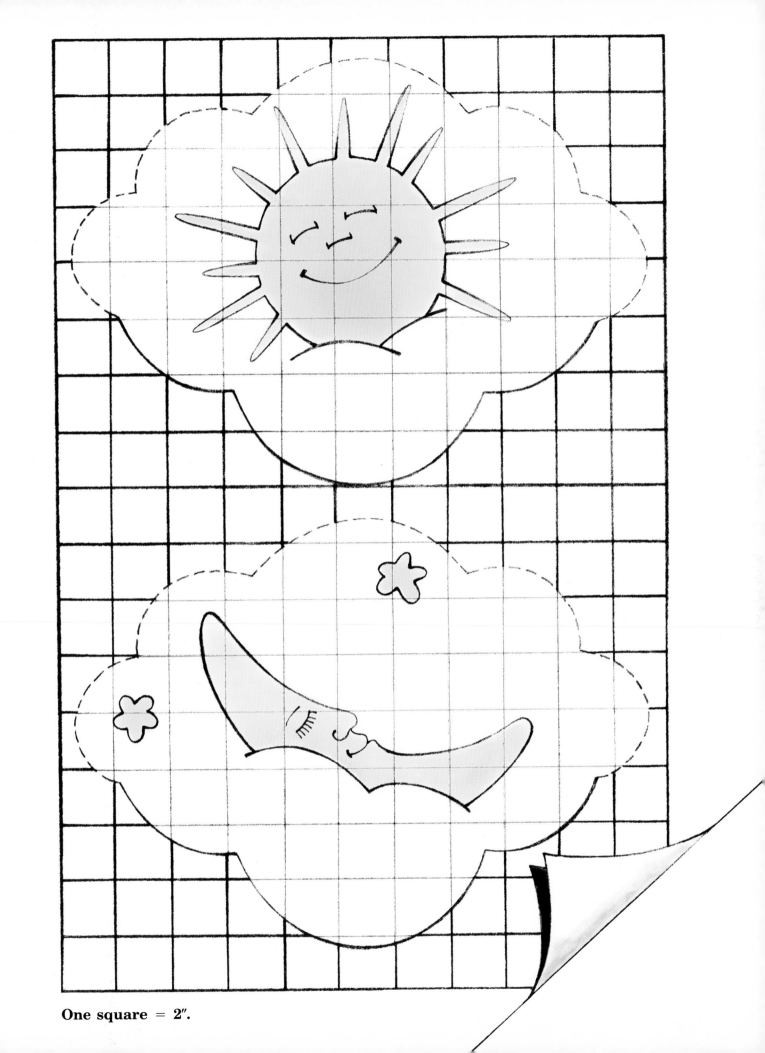

One square = 2″.

Sweet Dreams Pillowcase

You will need:
tracing paper
¼ yard (45"-wide) white fabric
12" x 23" piece of blue fabric
3" x 23" strip of yellow fabric
thread (white and blue)
tear-away backing for appliqué
blue embroidery thread (optional)

1. Trace and cut out the pattern for the border. From white fabric, cut two borders as marked. Using the water-soluble pen, write Sweet Dreams on one border, noting placement on pattern. Pin a piece of tear-away backing behind the letters. Embroider the letters by machine or hand, using satin stitch. Gently tear away the backing.

2. With right sides together and raw edges aligned, pin scalloped edge of borders and sew, stitching ¼" from the edge. Trim seam close to stitching; notch seam and clip Vs where scallops meet. Turn border right side out and press.

3. Fold the strip of yellow fabric with wrong sides and long edges together and press. With raw edges aligned, stack piece of blue fabric (right side up), yellow strip, and white border; sew, stitching ¼″ from the edge. Press borders away from blue fabric; press seam toward blue fabric. Topstitch blue fabric ¼″ from seam. Press yellow border toward blue fabric.

4. Fold the sewn piece with wrong sides and short edges together. Sew the raw edges, using ¼″ seam allowance. Trim seam close to stitching. Turn the pillowcase wrong side out. Finish edges by sewing again with ¼″ seam allowance. Turn pillowcase and press.

Sweet Dreams Quilt

You will need:
tracing paper
⅓ yard (45″-wide) white fabric
1⅓ yards (45″-wide) blue fabric
⅔ yard (45″-wide) yellow fabric
1 package of baby batting
thread (white and blue)
1⅔ yards (1″-wide) eyelet trim

1. Transfer pattern for the border to white fabric and cut two; trim one border as marked. From blue fabric, cut three 5¼″ x 20″ strips and one 24″ square (for backing). From yellow fabric, cut two 5¼″ x 20″ strips. Cut two 26″ x 28″ pieces of batting and treat these as one piece.

2. Position batting with short edge at top. Place one blue strip, right side up, at bottom corner of batting, aligning long and short edges. With right sides together, place one yellow strip on top of blue strip and sew as shown, stitching through three layers. (Figure A.) Open strips and press. Place a second blue strip on yellow and sew as before. (Figure B.)

Press strips open. Repeat procedure, sewing remaining yellow strip, then blue.

3. Trim batting at side and bottom edges of strips. (Do not trim batting at top of strips.) With right sides together and with ruffled edge of eyelet toward center of quilt, baste edge of eyelet to front of quilt along side and bottom edges. Place backing on top of quilt with right sides together and pin. Sew, using ¼″ seam allowance and being careful not to catch ruffled edge of eyelet in corners. Trim corners. Turn and lightly press the quilt.

4. Pin bottom edge of double-scalloped border to front of quilt about 3″ from top of strips, aligning Vs of scallops with seams of strips. Using a wide satin stitch, machine-appliqué the edge of the scallops to the quilt, sewing through all three layers. Trim strips to ¼″ above satin stitching, following line of stitching.

Turn straight edge of single-scalloped border under ½″ and press. With right sides together, align scallops on both borders and sew, using ¼″ seam allowance. Notch seam and clip Vs; turn border and press. Trim excess batting and backing to match scallops. Slip batting and backing inside scallops and slip-stitch straight edge of border to back of quilt.

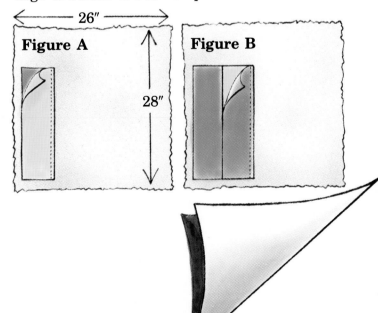

Quilt Border

Match Xs and continue pattern
across page.
Cut 2.

Pillowcase Border

Match Xs and continue pattern
across page.
Cut 2.

Sweet

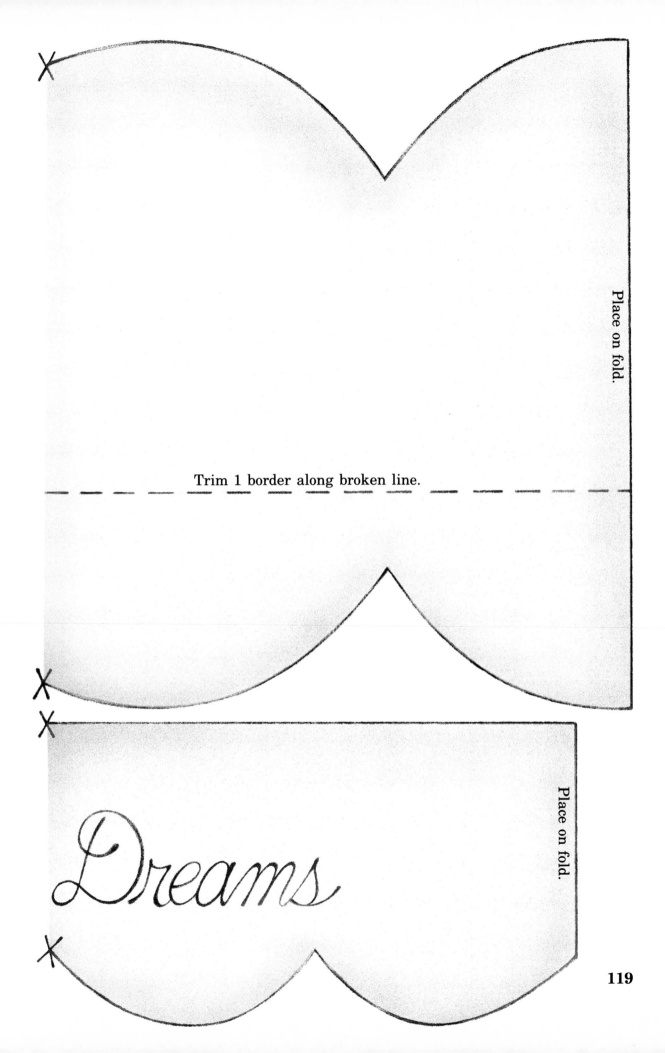

Trim 1 border along broken line.

Place on fold.

Place on fold.

Dreams

119

Designers & Contributors

Mims Adams, Traffic Stopper, 90.

Krista Brannon (age 9), Kitchen Cover-Up, 40.

Peyton Carmichael, A Frosty Family, 26; Bear Chair, 70; Paddle Ball Game, 108; Rock-A-Bye Cradle, 113.

Sharon A. Christman (and her fifth grade students, **Brooks Emory, Mary Crawford Owen,** and **Jenny Shaw**), A Bright Brigade, 22.

Karen C. Clenney, T-Shirt Sleepshirts, 88.

Brittany Copeland (age 13), Jiffy Jewelry, 47.

Kim Ann Crane, Surprise-in-a-Box, 12; Picture-Perfect Wreaths, 14; Daffy Doormouse, 24.

Hope H. Crawford, On Your Toes, 82; An Overall Great Idea, 92; Sweet Dreams Pillowcase and Quilt, 116.

Linda Hendrickson, Glitter Birds, 8; Waxen Wings, 18; Paper Penguins, 31; Busy Books, 42; Tabletop Tunes, 63; PJ Hideaway, 73; Lighthearted Long Johns, 80.

Zuelia Ann Hurt, Corner Cabin, 103.

Jo S. Kittinger, Leather-Look Desk Set, 52.

Mary Catharine Nicol, A Pudgy Pair, 55.

Lee and Dean Nix, Sitting Ducks, 60.

Walter M. Rush, Jr., construction of Bear Chair, 70, and Rock-A-Bye Cradle, 113.

Robin D. Snyder, Dream Cones, 10.

Linda Martin Stewart, Powder-Puff Snowmen, 4; Surprise-in-a-Box, 12; Cookie Cutter Cards, 34.

Kathleen A. Taylor, Sunbonnet Sheep, 66; What-to-Do Shoe, 94; Little Miss Molly, 98; Pigtail Jumprope, 110.

Carol Tipton, Shooting Stars, 85.

Madeline O'Brien White, Shiny Shapes, 6; How Dear!, 16; Cute 'n Curly Santa Wrap, 36; Scrappy Snowman Card, 38; Clown Bulletin Board, 44; Coupon Catcher, 50.

Special thanks to **Bair's Ski & Tennis** and **Chocolate Soup, Inc.,** of Birmingham, Alabama, for sharing their resources.